# A New Joy

# A New Joy

## Colleen Townsend Evans

**FLEMING H. REVELL COMPANY**

*Old Tappan, New Jersey*

Unless indicated otherwise, all Scripture quotations in this volume are from The New Testament in Modern English translated by J. B. Phillips, copyright © J. B. Phillips, 1958. Reprinted with permission of the Macmillan Company.

Scripture quotations identified KJV are from the King James Version of the Bible.

Quotations from *The Hiding Place* by Corrie ten Boom, copyright © 1971 by Corrie ten Boom and John and Elizabeth Sherrill, published by Chosen Books, are used by permission.

**Library of Congress Cataloging in Publication Data**

Evans, Colleen Townsend.
    A new joy.

    1.  Beatitudes.  2.  Woman—Religious life.
I.  Title.
BT382.E55     248′.843     73–3107
ISBN 0–8007–0590–4

# Gratefully. . . .

A moment ago I decided to write my acknowledgments — which may be a mistake at this time. You see, we are "packed" into our favorite spot in the high Sierra . . . the experience of being here as a family and the outrageous beauty that surrounds us make me feel grateful to everyone and everything. The Sierra are heady wine for me, and as a result these acknowledgments may be much longer than they would have been had I written them in the city. But here goes. . . .

First, my family. . . . I once heard of a man who dedicated a book to "my family, without whose help this would have been done in half the time." Ah, yes — but on the other hand, without my family's encouragement, interest, and inspiration I never would have begun writing this book. A casual "Hey, Mom — how're you doing on your thing?" from one of the boys . . . or a daughter who was not only willing to listen, but was always genuinely interested, meant more to me than they will ever know.

Then, my friends . . . those who prayed . . . those who urged me on and listened to what I read them. You know who you are, and how much I appreciate your help.

Then, the people and the books (other than the Scriptures) that have shaped my thinking on the Beatitudes. . . . My husband's commentaries were always so helpful to me in my study . . . Dr. Ralph Sockman's *The Higher Happiness* was filled with his deep insights . . . so often I found my own thoughts and feelings paralleling his. . . . Dr. J. B. Phillips's paraphrase of the Sermon on the Mount, my favorite translation and the one used in this book.

And then, the women in that first study group in the Bel Air church . . . sharing so much of themselves as we paraphrased and applied to

5

our own lives these powerful words of Jesus. What a fellowship we had as we studied, labored, and loved together. Thank you, gals!

And now you, Phyllis . . . surely, this book would never have been completed without your persistence and your gifts. Though we have only been together three times, you are a "soul sister." We "feel" together, and in the deepest sense it has been a joy to work with you. You have taken my little scraps of paper, my bundles of pages written in longhand fifty pages at a time, and with your editorial skills brought order out of chaos. I don't know how to thank you, Phyllis, but as you always seem to know how I feel — please know now.

Now, one final acknowledgment. (I warned you this would be long!) There are many who have taught me and nurtured me in my faith since I started on the Way. To them I am continually grateful. But there are those who were my friends *before* I started on the Way — and they stuck by me even though my ready answers and do-it-yourself faith must have been discouraging to them. They never pushed or preached — they simply shared their new faith in Christ with me in such a winsome way that — well, what else could I do? And so, to them — to that contagiously joyful group of young people — now not so young, but still spreading and keeping the faith in their own way . . . at Synanon House in California, in a classroom at Princeton University, in a psychologist's office, in homes, and in pulpits across the land — to them, a Thank You that leaps from my heart.

One of that group not only helped to start me on the Way . . . in God's grace he chose to walk it with me. I too chose him — and I choose him now. And so this book is dedicated . . .

TO Louie

# Contents

# Preface

I have just come in from a walk along the beach. It was cold today, so my nose is red and my body tingles. What a wonderful, beautiful feeling!

Walking the beach is something I love, but that isn't all. I need it. It isn't something I do every day for exercise. No, I save the beach for days when I need the sea's ministry. For there are times when I need the wind—like the wind of the Spirit—to blow the cobwebs from my mind and let me think more clearly. And there are times when the vastness of the sea reminds me of the vastness of God's love, and the tide's ebb and flow of His dependability.

One night I walked the beach until dawn seeking the strength I needed to face surgery—for some reason a thing I found particularly difficult at that time. Why? I asked myself. Then the words of my doctor-friend came to my mind, giving me a clue: "I think we'll find everything in good order, Coke, but we can't be sure."

It was fear, not of surgery but of the unknown, that tormented me. Over and over I told myself it was a common enough fear, but it numbed me. Release came only when I allowed myself to remember that God can even be—can *especially* be—trusted with the unknowns of our lives.

How many times my husband Lou and I have been drawn to the sea when we needed guidance on specific issues in our

church or in our own lives. We realize that God is everywhere
and always within our reach, so that we don't have to go to a
particular place to talk to Him. It's just that we can get away
from life's distractions when we walk the quiet beach where
nothing interrupts our conversation. It isn't God who needs
the silence — *we* do.

So it has gone — walks, too many to count, during these past
several years when we have had the privilege of living along-
side the sea. And so it was today. I needed to think, to sort
things out in my mind, for I had been asked a question I
didn't know how to answer.

When a person writes a book, he usually includes a preface
explaining the purpose of the book. Well, I had written a
book, and now Fleming H. Revell Company, my publishers,
asked me for a preface. In other words, my readers would be
asking me, "Why did you write this book?" The question was
simple enough. Not so the answer.

I suppose I could say I wrote the book because I was asked
to. A few years ago I wrote an article for *Guideposts* entitled
"Express Your True Feelings." It was based on the Beatitude
"Happy are the utterly sincere, for they will see God" (Matthew
5:8). Revell suggested that I write a book about all the Beatitudes, and I liked the idea. But that isn't the whole story, and
the book didn't really begin there.

It began many years ago and certainly not as a book. It was
a study, a simple, feeling-level study, that grew out of my own
life. In those days I was a young wife and the mother of four
little children. Although I had been a Christian only a few
years, my life had been very glowing and exciting — up to that
time. But with the responsibilities and work of a family comes
fatigue, and one morning I woke up wondering where the
glow had gone.

I began to think back a few years, searching for an answer.
Yes, it was there all right — at first I could see it dimly, but
gradually the visibility improved.

For several years before I married Louie I had worked in

the motion picture industry. I thoroughly enjoyed my career
and especially the people with whom I worked. During those
years I also became a very enthusiastic believer in Jesus Christ.
To me it didn't seem unusual that a spiritual rebirth should
happen to someone in my profession—I have known, and
still know, many dedicated Christians in the motion picture
industry. But to many people the combination of my belief
and my profession had a special attraction. Because of that I
was often asked to speak to various groups, telling them how
Christ came into my life. Even after I left my motion picture
work for my "other career," the one I wanted more, the
speaking invitations continued.

Because I have always been eager to share my faith, I said
yes to as many requests as I could, although speaking was not
then (and is not now) a thing I leap toward with joy. Eventually the pressure became uncomfortable because I allowed
myself to be influenced by a few people who felt that it was
not only my opportunity but my duty to speak about Jesus
publicly.

Yes, I could see where the glow had gone. It had retreated
to deep inside me. I was beginning to feel like an "up front"
Christian and obviously I was resisting the celebrity bit. It is
one thing to talk about being a Christian in front of groups,
but quite another to be a Christian in your home and in your
community. I longed to be more deeply Christian where it
really counted, but I needed help.

God has a marvelous sense of timing. At the very moment
when I really needed it, I decided to join a women's Bible-
study group in the new church we were starting in Bel Air,
California. I did it simply to learn more about the Bible,
never expecting that it would offer me anything more.

Our group met once a week, exploring several different
methods of studying the Bible. Then, after dealing with the
historical and theological background of a passage, we were
asked to rewrite it in our own words, forgetting everything
but what the passage meant to each of us, personally. As I did

that, the Scriptures suddenly became very real. I'll never forget the excitement I felt when I began to see that the Bible could be applied to life today—and especially to *my* life.

But why a book about the Beatitudes? I chose them because in these words Jesus was speaking to believers like me—they weren't very pious and they were far from perfect, but they had decided *for* Jesus. Now they needed His help in trying to live the life to which He had called them.

Help is exactly what you will find in the Beatitudes, for here is where Jesus spells out His gospel of love. He tells us what love is, how it feels, and what it does. Instead of listing laws and commandments, He explains how our inner motivations and heart responses can either help us express love or get in its way. Specifically, practically, and in such a down-to-earth manner, Jesus gets to the core of the Christian life.

That was what I needed several years ago, and so my study of the Beatitudes began. I wanted to find out what these beautiful words meant when Jesus spoke them almost two thousand years ago—and what they might mean to me, a woman living in our complicated modern world.

I immersed myself in Matthew 5, eventually becoming familiar with the Sermon on the Mount in every translation I could find. Gradually I could feel what it must have been like to be in that crowd of believers at Jesus' feet. I could see myself among them as I wrote a paraphrase of what I thought Jesus might have said to me had I been alone with Him that day. Finally, and perhaps more important than anything else, I prayed that the *attitudes* Jesus described might become a part of me, from the inside out.

Because it helps me to write down my thoughts and feelings, I began to record the practical applications of the Beatitudes as they came to me. Sometimes they would come during moments of meditation and prayer, but more often they came unexpectedly as I was rushing from place to place doing my thing for the day. And so, this book has been written on scraps of paper as I waited for the car pool to take my children to school or as I took my turn as driver and waited outside the school, on the program for a play, or on the back of a church bulletin when I was struck with an idea in church. (Forgive me, Louie!) My children are now teen-agers and therefore the jottings shared here cover the musings and feelings of years.

But—back to the question I considered as I walked the beach this morning. Why did I write this book at all? By now you know, just as I do. I wrote it out of my own need. I wrote it because I have found the Bible—and here, specifically, the Beatitudes—to be real and vital to me, a woman living today. I am sharing in this way because during the past few years I have learned that sharing our needs, our struggles, our joys, our affirmations, our love—in short, sharing ourselves—can be one of life's richest experiences. And so I am receiving perhaps more than my share.

If, through this book, I can help one woman discover that Jesus Christ is real, and that His Word is something she can use in her everyday life, I shall be forever grateful.

These pages are not about talking the talk, but about walking the walk. And now, I'll shake the sand from my shoes and get on with it.

COLLEEN TOWNSEND EVANS

# 1

---

**Happy are the humble-minded, for the kingdom of Heaven is theirs!**

Matthew 5:3 PHILLIPS

**Blessed are the poor in spirit: for theirs is the kingdom of heaven.**

Matthew 5:3 KJV

# The Humble Women

Poor . . . I can't imagine anyone *wanting* to be poor . . . to be totally destitute, in need, anxious, hopeless, frightened. . . . Surely our loving Lord doesn't want this for us?

And yet, Jesus says that only if we are poor will we be happy. . . . "Blessed are the poor in spirit: for theirs is the kingdom of heaven."

There were many poor people sitting at Jesus' feet when He spoke these words, and He wasn't telling them that they never had it so good. No—Jesus had great compassion for human need, and the sight of the suffering poor grieved Him. Obviously He was talking about something beyond physical need.

All right . . . suppose I were in the crowd that came to hear

Him speak—and suppose I were poor. . . . I wouldn't have come to get food—He had none. I wouldn't have come for money—He had none. But perhaps I would have come because I needed something else, something that only Jesus could give me.

Yes—now there seems to be new meaning in the word *poor*. I was thinking of it in terms of the kind of poverty we're trying to eliminate from our world . . . starvation, disease, ignorance. But there is another kind of poverty—one that is much worse and not as visible. There is a poverty of the spirit. And that's what Jesus is talking about in the first Beatitude.

"Blessed are the poor in spirit. . . ." This seems to be the center from which the other Beatitudes radiate. For unless we know how poor we are without Christ, we'll never reach out for Him. If we feel we can take care of ourselves, why ask for help—even from God?

Come to think of it, the happiest people I know are those who have tried and failed—even hit bottom—and then reached out for help. Realizing their spiritual bankruptcy, they asked Jesus to take over their lives. They entered the kingdom through the door of their own need, and they were met by God's grace.

They're not only the happiest but the freest people I've known . . . free to be, to love, and to let God work through them. They enjoy each moment, with no regrets for yesterday and no worries about tomorrow. They don't have to prove anything—they work because they *want* to, not because the world *expects* it of them. To me, these people are very rich—not necessarily in material things, but in the things of the spirit. They possess the peace and joy that come from walking close to God. And yet, this route to the kingdom begins with the painful admission that we are poor and needy.

For me it began during my mid-teens when, without actually seeking it, I had an experience that was both mystical and profound. One evening when I was alone, I went to my room—and found myself in the presence of a blinding white light. It was all around me . . . overwhelming, consuming. I was part of it and it was part of me. At the core of my being—in my spirit—I felt free and peaceful. I was aware of my one-ness with all things, all people—and especially with God.

Ever since that moment I have never doubted the reality of God or His presence in our human lives. Although that experience wasn't repeated, I still have the strength and assurance it gave me. That was the beginning of my conscious spiritual journey.

For many years I didn't mention that evening to anyone except my mother. In fact, even now I wonder about sharing such an intensely personal incident, for I think we are in trouble when we base our faith upon experience or feeling alone. And yet, what we have seen and heard and touched is a valid part of ourselves. For me, that moment was where my pilgrimage began.

In the years that followed I held fast to my faith in God, allowing Him to influence my life but not to guide it. . . . I could do that myself. Then, during my college years, I began to feel a gnawing hunger—there *had* to be more to life than what I saw on the surface. We *had* to do more than go through the motions. There *had* to be meaning, warmth, closeness, love. I was hungry for more of God in my life . . . but I didn't know where to find Him.

Up to that point my relationship with established religion had been casual . . . I had wandered in and out of church. Now I looked to the church to show me the way to God. I joined, I worked, I tithed, I tried—and I found only frustration and weariness. The route of "churchianity" was not for me.

By that time I had gone from college to Hollywood where I was put under contract to a motion picture studio and promised a creative career. I thoroughly enjoyed my work . . . it was fun, exciting, and lucrative—and I loved the people! Materially, my background had been very simple, and for the first time in my life I had some of the things I always thought I wanted . . . plus glamorous surroundings, stimulating work, and talented people. Yet underneath the surface of my being—deep down in my spirit—my possessions added up to zero. I had more of everything, but "everything" was not enough. The gnawing hunger was still there.

I felt poor—and in a way that had nothing to do with anything external. My poverty was on the inside. True, I had been aware of my spiritual needs for months, but now the needs were greater. Before, there was always something I could do about them—work harder, try harder, search further. Not anymore . . . I had run out of things to do . . . I had done them all and I was exhausted. And what good were all my efforts? Where did they get me? Spiritually I was bankrupt. Let someone else try.

Someone did. At that most needful time in my life I met a group of young new Christians. They were such warm, real people, and I felt myself being drawn toward their loving concern for me. They became my friends, and I began to hear what they were saying about God.

My friends told me that God was real . . . but I already knew that. They said there is a God-sized vacuum in each of us, and until it is filled with God we will never have true peace . . . I was beginning to know that. But then they told me something I had never known—they told me how to find God!

They said I wouldn't find Him by doing good or by working harder.

They said I wouldn't find Him through any efforts of my own.

They said I would find Him through a Person . . . through

a Person so much like myself that He would understand my needs, yet Someone so thoroughly *God* that He could feed my hungry spirit.

At last I understood. At last I had been shown the Way. My friends urged me to follow it . . . to give Jesus my impoverished life and let Him make something useful out of it. And so I did. It was quiet . . . and simple . . . and very, very real. I said yes to Jesus Christ . . . and the God I had known to be real—but far away—came into my life.

What a difference there is between a vague sort of faith and a personal relationship with a living Christ! He has given me direction and a goal—and nothing has ever been quite the same for me. If I had to describe in a few words how my life has been changed by becoming a Christian, I would borrow these words from Jesus: "The man who wants to save his life will lose it; but the man who loses his life for my sake will find it" (Matthew 16:25).

Left to ourselves, we find this world a lonely place. No matter how many friends we have, or how big the family, we feel cut off from a warmth and love we can't describe. . . . It's always "out there somewhere"—until we open our hearts and let the Holy Spirit "in here." He is a part of God Himself, and He will keep us company as long as we live on this earth.

In our kingdom-walk we are receivers—doers, too, but receivers first. Yet not all of us accept God's gifts. Some people, because of their pride, cannot reach out and take them. They resent God—and they are never happy.

Pride lives a very narrow life. It must have all the answers and insists on having its own way. It talks too much. It has trouble getting along with people . . . it is prejudiced . . . its ego is so big, you can't help bumping into it. Pride wants too much and offers too little.

Humility is just the opposite . . . its life is full and active.

Humility is smart enough to know we can't know everything. It listens, and looks at life through the eyes of others. Humility has many friends because it has time and space in its life for more than itself . . . the door to its heart is never locked. Humility is thankful for all it has, and because it has received so much, it gives unendingly.

Humility opens the way to God and happiness. Pride stands back, hands at its sides, and says, "No, thanks, I can do it myself." Humility is free to admit its need for God and others and comes with hands outstretched.

Thinking about humility reminds me of two wonderful people we met in Edinburgh many years ago. Louie and I had gone to Scotland so that he could complete his graduate studies at New College. We had spent summers in work camps overseas, but this time we were to be away from our country and our family for two years—and we were expecting our first child.

Louie's advisor and New Testament teacher was Professor James Stewart, a man well known as a New Testament scholar and a powerful preacher. We went to hear him preach at St. George's West on our first Sunday in Edinburgh, and after the service we stayed in our seats for a long time, savoring the inspiration his words had given us. He was a man small in stature and gigantic in spirit—a man of natural talents, a disciplined mind, and the power uniquely born of the Holy Spirit in a life. We were so grateful that Louie was to learn from this man for the next two years.

As great as he was in the pulpit, Professor Stewart was even more impressive as a human being . . . and in the gentlest, most humane way. We might have felt homesick those first months had it not been for the many kindnesses he and his lovely wife, Rosamund, sent our way.

They came to see me in the hospital when our son Dan was born six weeks earlier than expected. They invited us to spend

Christmas with them and their family, realizing that this was the first time we were away from home for the holidays. And then there were the evenings we and our fellow students spent at their house, drinking Ros's good tea and asking questions of Professor Stewart late into the night. . . . And Ros pedaling over to our flat on her bicycle with flowers picked from her garden, arriving just in time for a "wee visit" while I nursed the "bairn." (We had a baby a year in Scotland, so there was always a bairn.)

The "gift" that meant the most to us came when little Dan was six weeks old. By that time Louie was filling the pulpit in a little country church in Penicuik every Sunday, and we wanted to have our son baptized there. Louie, as Dan's father, couldn't perform the service—and of course you can guess who we *wanted* to do it. But we just didn't have the nerve to ask.

Getting to Penicuik wasn't easy. It meant a forty-five-minute ride through the Pentland hills—in the middle of winter. A car in postwar Britain was a luxury few of us could afford, and so we took a long, bumpy ride on a bus. It was too much to ask . . . warm and generous as Professor Stewart was, he was still a very busy man. A friend of ours offered to do the service and we gratefully accepted.

On the morning of Dan's baptism, I dressed him in his warmest and best, and the four of us took the long bus ride to Penicuik. It was cold and the roads were icy, so the ride was longer than usual. When we arrived at the church I was taken to the vestry. Then, at the appropriate moment in the service, I was led down the aisle, holding Dan in my arms. Out of the corner of my eye I thought I recognized a man sitting in the rear of the church. After the sacrament, I turned to walk back down the aisle and this time I got a better look. I had been right the first time—it *was* Professor Stewart! Hearing one of our friends mention that Dan was going to be baptized, he had come all the way out on the bus by himself to be there. After the service he slipped away as quietly as he came. *But he had been there.* In that act, and in countless others like it, he and Ros taught me more about the Christian life and attitude than all his sermons put together. Truly they are two who walk humbly with their Lord.

To be poor in spirit is to be in touch with our own need. It's uncomfortable . . . that's why our own spiritual need must be filled before we can touch the needs of others. Before we can appreciate the worth of another human being, we must feel that we ourselves are of value. And many of us don't.

It's a funny thing about pride . . . often it's a cover-up for a low opinion of the self. It's a way of saying, "All right, world, I know nobody can love me — so I'll look after myself!" It doesn't even give God a chance.

I have a friend, a very lovely person, who only a few years ago had so little feeling of self-worth that she almost called it quits. She was so desperately in need of self-respect that she was completely unable to give to others. Margot even found it difficult to function as wife and mother, but she covered up her sense of deficiency with a layer of pride. None of us realized how empty she felt inside.

One day Margot felt a mysterious stirring within her. Gently, but persistently, it pushed against her pride until it cracked . . . without quite understanding what she was doing, Margot reached out for help. She began coming to church for counseling, and when her minister realized how deep her feelings of unworthiness were, he persuaded her to see a sensitive, caring psychiatrist.

It's wonderful how God uses time and people. For many long, tiring months the minister and the psychiatrist worked with Margot and through them God was able to bring about a healing in her life.

Margot was driving home from the psychiatrist's office one day after a session that had been a breakthrough . . . a moment when the light of understanding broke through to her darkened spirit. As she drove through the park she began to feel warmed by that inner light and suddenly she found herself saying, "Margot, you're a precious person . . . you're special." Over and over she said it until she began to cry. She pulled over, stopped the car and sat basking in a wonderful new awareness of God's love for her.

When Margot started the car to drive home, she did something significant. She reached down and fastened her seat belt. She had never done that before. She had never cared enough about herself before. Now, in one simple action, she was saying, "God cares for me . . . and *I* care."

Margot was beginning a whole new life that was totally different from anything she had known. Love—God's love— transformed her into a generous and thoughtful person. Being able to receive made her able to give . . . and as she looked around she saw how much she was needed. At last she could look beyond herself to others.


A Christian walks humbly with his Lord, or he doesn't walk the Way. Humility itself can become proud—proud of being loved, proud of serving, proud of achieving. That's when Jesus reminds us of our poverty . . . to keep us humble, He takes us through one of life's many Valleys of Humiliation.

I don't know how to avoid these valleys—there are no detours along the Way. And I don't like what I just wrote—but I believe it.

Many years ago Louie and I wanted to go to Africa. Louie had been there earlier and he had lost his heart to it. I liked what he told me about the country, and especially about the people. In America we have so many external things that our hands do not easily reach out to receive what God offers. But in the Third World, where people have had to struggle and suffer through disease, famine, and poverty, there seems to be a willingness—even an eagerness—to reach out and accept God's grace. The reports we've recently received from friends in these areas thrill us as we hear that Christ is becoming Lord to millions. And even back then, that was where we wanted to work!

Hopefully, we offered ourselves—once in the beginning of our ministry and again several years later. Each time the door closed gently but firmly, and finally we got the message— "Keep serving where you are."

And where were we? Right smack in the middle of affluent America!

Don't get me wrong—it's not that I feel a person has to be economically poor to be humble. Some of the most humble people I know are in our present congregation—and they would be considered affluent. But material wealth *can* blind us to the needs of the deprived . . . exclusive, gracious living *can* make us forget those who know of the gracious life only from movies and TV . . . built-in security *can* make us insensitive to those who have to worry about how they will pay their bills all their lives. Worst of all, more than enough *can* make us forget that we always need Christ.

Gradually we began to understand the meaning in the door that closed . . . we have come to see the areas we serve as bursting with potential for God. We are grateful for the challenge, and truly humbled by it. But make no mistake about it —there are many Valleys of Humiliation in the City of Affluence. We've been through some of them.

I especially remember being installed into the ministry of one of our churches. Our friend, the Reverend James Jones, was giving the charge to Louie when he pointed a finger at us and said, "I have a feeling that in this place you will have to decrease so that Christ can increase."

They were hard words for us to hear, but Jim was right. In

fact, he was prophetic. Through the years Christ *has* increased . . . and there *have* been valleys for us, many of them. But there has also been joy, joy in the fulfilling of the promise that "Every valley shall be exalted . . ." (Isaiah 40:4 KJV). It has often been painful for us to be put in touch with our own spiritual need, but it has brought us—and kept us—close to God. And believe me, that *is* happiness!

Yes, I'm ready now to go on to the other Beatitudes, Jesus. I need Your gifts so very much, and so I'm going with my hands open and outstretched. I want to learn what it means to be a Christian in the deepest sense. I want to become the kind of person You can use.

*Happy is the woman who knows that without God she is nothing . . . but that with God working through her, she has the strength and power of His love. This woman will be quick to sense longing in the human spirit, and where there is need she will nourish it. Her humility will come from the very center of her being, and it will never allow her to look down on anyone—not even on people who look down on people. . . . And because her humility is real, she will know a bit of heaven right here on earth.*

# 2

Happy are those who know what sorrow means, for they will be given courage and comfort!

Matthew 5:4 PHILLIPS

Blessed are they that mourn: for they shall be comforted.

Matthew 5:4 KJV

# The Sorrowing Women

It's hard for me to think about mourning, Jesus. Mourning is so painful, I just can't see how any kind of happiness can come of it.

And yet You say it will. . . . You're telling us—*urging* us—to mourn, to sorrow, so there must be something good in it for us, something beyond the pain. Then I must look further . . . until I understand this Beatitude. It's important.

*To mourn* . . . what does it mean? To give way? to bend? to break? Webster says simply, "To feel or express sorrow." That helps a little, and it makes sense. To mourn is to *feel* pain, to allow it to penetrate us, not to brace ourselves against it. It means we can't pick and choose only the parts of

life that we like and reject the rest. No, if we are to experience life truly, deeply, and realistically, we must be
vulnerable to all of life . . . not only its joys, but its sorrows
as well.

But there's more, much more, to mourning. Even Webster
suggests that the feeling of sorrow is not enough. We must
express it, let it pass through us. And do we? How often I
have heard people say, "Share your joys, but keep your sorrows to yourself." I think I know what they mean—no one
likes to be around a person who wallows in self-pity, using
sorrow as a means of attracting attention. But that's sickness,
not mourning.

The heart was never meant to be a prison for pain. When
we stifle an honest expression of real sorrow, we're denying
part of our humanity. And if we are Jesus followers, we're
denying His promise: "Happy are those who know what sorrow means, for they will be given courage and comfort."

The words of this Beatitude are simple, but their implica-
tion is deep and sound. It means that there *can* be comfort for
our sorrows, but only if we face loss, fear, and anxiety
squarely. When we allow ourselves to feel the pain of mourning, then we can be healed.

Somehow many of us Christians have come to believe just
the opposite. We think that if we become truly spiritual the
blows of life will not reach us; and that if they do, we will
have the power to rise above them instantly. Is this really
true? Does Christianity offer some kind of holy immunity
against grief and pain? And does "living victoriously" mean
living beyond fear, discouragement, loneliness, and desola-
tion? I wonder . . . I really wonder. If it's true, then the
Beatitude is false—and we know it is not.

Jesus is telling us to feel everything. To be spiritually alive
is not to be dead to hurt and pain, but to be free to experience
them, trusting God to bring us through them safely.

We need the dark nights, sleepless and agonizing as they are. We need the hurts that keep us tender and the unexplained sorrows that stretch our faith and trust. Living through them will make us different people—and the difference can be good!

Many years ago I spent a summer working as a volunteer, helping to build a refugee camp on the outskirts of Paris. I worked side by side with men and women who had been victims of a war, and as we came to know each other as friends their stories gradually tumbled out. They had lived through unbelievable terror and persecution, and although their dark night had passed, the fact that they had suffered would always be a part of their lives. Clearly they were different from the rest of us—sorrow had taught them what was really important in life. It had made them extremely sensitive to other people's needs. They gave instead of asking, they comforted when others complained. They were some of the most understanding, expressive human beings I have ever met. And through them I learned how God works through our dark nights, using them to deepen the shallow areas of our lives.

Then it's right for Christians to mourn, isn't it, Jesus? Is that what You're telling us in this Beatitude? Are You saying that, as Christians, we should feel *more* of life, not less? Yes, I think I understand. Unless we open ourselves up to pain and hurt and loss, You cannot heal us . . . for by shutting out the sorrow, we shut You out, too.

You knew the dark nights . . . many of them. And when You felt something, You didn't try to hide it. When Your friend Lazarus died, You cried, just the way I cry when a good friend is gone. It's not that I think I won't see my friend again—for I believe in Your heaven—but I will miss her here on earth.

In our church, which is quite large, we are in touch with death thirty or forty times a year. Still I find it hard to accept its frequency and finality. Part of me rejoices, knowing that death opens a door to an existence far more beautiful than I can comprehend. But another part of me — the here-and-now, earthy part — finds it hard to accept the physical separation and the sense of loss. Having known and loved the person, I mourn.

And when I mourn I am filled with pain that seems unbearable at first. But only at first. It doesn't go away quickly — in fact, it doesn't go away at all. It changes . . . as it pushes back the walls of my resistance to death, the pain itself is softened. Sometimes it turns to tears, and sometimes to quiet moments of reflection. It doesn't matter which. The important thing is that I am made vulnerable, receptive — to more pain? Perhaps, but certainly to God's healing love. And Jesus, who knew the human longing for a departed friend, makes the pain bearable and the loss understandable.

But sorrow can be a hardening experience as well. I have a friend who lost someone very close to her, and while many of us tried to comfort her, she wasn't open to a helping hand, human or divine. Somewhere in her childhood she had been taught to hide her feelings, especially the sad ones, and today, more than a year after her tragic loss, she is still unreachable. The pain inside her has grown in upon itself and become a kind of spiritual malignancy. The iron will that locks it in, locks the healing out.

Recently I learned that my friend is in the hospital and I'm concerned about her. If only she could unlock her heart and let the hurt, the loneliness, and the bitterness out into the open where Jesus could apply His healing light. Then perhaps she could share her grief with a friend — for God uses people in His healing process, too, and there are many who

care. I pray she will — oh, how I pray she will! But the decision is hers. The lock on the door of my friend's heart is on
the inside, and only she can open it.

How different the experience of mourning has been in the
life of another good friend. Mary and Joel Stein were two of
the most beautiful people I've ever known. They met and
married a little later than most couples and were blessed with
an immense capacity to enjoy each other. I knew them
through my work when I was a single career girl, and I don't
think they ever realized how much inspiration I found just
being in their home. Joel was quite a powerful man in our
field, but he was even more successful as a human being . . .
so warm, open, communicative, and real. His wife Mary was
a vivacious, outgoing woman who deserved him in every way.
In an industry not known for happy marriages, theirs was an
uncommonly good one.

For many years the Steins were childless. Then Mary gave
birth to a son who brought new meaning and joy to their
very happy home. And suddenly it was over. There wasn't
even a warning. One day Joel had a heart attack and a few
hours later he was gone. Everybody who knew and loved him
was shocked, but Mary's loss seemed unbearable. She was a
strong-minded person who always seemed able to face anything in life . . . but could she face death?

I was with Mary soon after Joel died, and I'll never forget
what she said: "Oh, Colleen, life will never be the same without him." I wondered whether she would be able to go on
with life at all. . . . How I longed to share her suffering, to
bring some rest to the tired, sleepless eyes. But I could only
wait . . . and pray . . . and hope.

I couldn't help asking myself whether Joel's death would
have been more bearable if Mary had been prepared for it . . .
perhaps a lingering illness softens the final blow? But as I and
Mary's other friends watched her go through her dark night,

we realized that death—whenever it comes, however it comes—is a stunning, rending loss.

Death will come to all of us, and to all we know and love. Yet it's only a word, never real, until it strikes close to us. There is nothing we can do beforehand to lessen its pain. It will pass through us or remain forever outside us waiting to get in. It will not go away.

Is mourning cruel? Yes, terribly. But God doesn't bring it upon us as a punishment or a toughening process. Mourning is part of our human condition. Because we can love—and because we need love—we must get close to other human beings. Our lives touch and mingle . . . we add to each other . . . and when a loved one is torn away, our love bleeds. That is mourning.

If there were some preventive spiritual medicine we could take ahead of time to lessen the pain and shorten the long days and weeks and months of sorrow—what then? Mourning would be simply an event that occurred, an obstacle along our way, but nothing that left its mark upon us. No happiness could possibly come of it, for we would never reach the second part of the Beatitude—God's refining, deepening, life-changing comfort.

I understood that when I watched Mary struggle with her pain. Gradually the confusion began to sort itself out and she felt some of her former strength returning. She had been right—life *wouldn't* be the same for her without Joel. Not ever. But God, working through the love and warmth of Mary's friends, helped her to see that life was still good. That appreciation was something she wanted to pass on to her son. And she did. Because she left herself open to sorrow—yet never indulged herself in it—she found Someone to share it with her. Then, when she was strong enough, she was able to lift the burden of grief from her child.

Fern, another very special friend of mine, was a different

kind of woman. Quiet, soft-spoken, vulnerable, her whole
existence revolved around her young doctor-husband. They
were happy, they had much to look forward to . . . and then
Tom was gone and there was nothing left. Or so it seemed
to Fern. Later she told me about those terrible days.

At first there was shock, a refusal to believe that Tom was
dead. Then there was contempt for the life that lay ahead
of her, a life she didn't want to live. For besides Fern's loneliness, there were practical problems to face . . . two children
to support, her husband's aging mother to care for, very little
money, no job, and no training for one.

Even worse was the call from the tomb, the visits to the
graveside again and again. "I was like the women who went
to Christ's tomb, weeping and carrying spices, expecting to
minister to His body," Fern said. "But you remember how the
angel met them at the tomb and told them that Jesus wasn't
there? In a way, that's what happened to me. One day I began
to cry, and that was the beginning of my letting go of sorrow.
I could feel God standing close to me and I knew that my tears
were part of His therapy. He came to me through them, because then He could get at my pain."

Fern realized that she had to make a decision. If she truly
believed in God's promise of comfort, she had to trust Him
completely. She had to depend on Him to give her the courage
to face life again. Of course she couldn't do it herself . . .
and that's why the future had looked so impossibly difficult to
her. She never could have found her way alone in such darkness. But she didn't have to . . . there was a Light. . . . And
oh, what an eager receiver she was! She not only accepted the
Light, she absorbed it . . . it became part of her.

"God brings us comfort in so many ways," Fern said. "I
could see Him reaching out to heal me through other people
. . . in a handshake, in a smile, or a single word. And then
one day, after another sleepless night, I saw Him in the
sunrise—and I realized then that I had forgotten that the

sun *does* rise every day. I had been looking only at the sunsets.

"At last I could commit Tom to God and stop being a
tomb-looker. I knew that eventually I would be able to feel
joy because my husband was in the presence of the Risen
Lord. It was as if the stone of sorrow, like the stone closing
Christ's tomb, had been rolled aside and I could see that God
was there."

It was time for Fern to go on in life. We all knew it because
we could feel God working through us to help her. First
there was a job—a job she could handle and one that gave her
room to grow. Then there were friends and family to help
care for the children and Tom's mother, giving Fern time to
adjust to the demands of a home and a job.

Finally there was joy—joy in her memories of a wonderful
life with Tom . . . recalling the happy times they shared, the
struggles that brought them closer and deepened their love
. . . anticipation of the reunion they would have someday.

Fern never pitied herself, never became morbid on holidays or on the anniversary of Tom's death. "God wants us
to celebrate life," she said. "And Tom isn't dead."

Neither is Fern. There is a lot of life for her to live. And
she has become strong enough for others to lean on in their
time of grief. In fact, she has become a great blessing in our
congregation by helping many to turn away from the tomb.
How often I have heard that Fern has helped someone turn
the corner . . . going with that person to the graveside, helping to pray these simple, sorrow-touched words:

Oh, God, let this sorrow that has come upon me be to Your
    glory,
and reveal Yourself to others through it. . . .
I accept it, Lord. . . . Let Your name be glorified through it.

Fern came through her dark night because she opened
herself up to its pain. She mourned—more deeply than anyone I have ever known—and she was comforted by a loving

God. She has truly lived this Beatitude, and I have seen happiness — hers and others' — come out of sorrow. I believe.

Death is not the only human experience that ushers mourning into our lives. In the summer, when our family goes traveling, we often contact old friends — some from college or seminary days, some from previous pastorates, and some I worked with years ago. It's wonderful to see them, and within a few short hours we always manage to catch up on the years of living. That's the way it is with good friends.

We're happy when we find our friends growing, stretching, and enjoying God's good life, and we celebrate with them. But sometimes we come upon friends in mourning, and it's not always death that lays them low. One friend may mourn a marriage broken after twenty-five years. Another mourns for an adult daughter stubbornly pursuing a course of life that will ultimately hurt her and others. Another is recovering from the loss of a breast in a mastectomy, and realistically facing what this means to a woman . . . she mourns over the physical, emotional, and psychological shock to her very feminine being.

As our friends honestly expose their pain to us and to God, as they open up and become vulnerable to Him, His light and love begin to do what only they can do . . . they heal. We have seen it happen, even in the midst of pain. As one friend said, "It hurts like crazy, but I'm beginning to feel this unexplainable peace — it has to be from God." And of course it is.

Very often there is nothing we can do beyond mourning. Like Jesus weeping over Lazarus' death, we must wait for comfort and the strength to go on. But there are other times when mourning is only the beginning of something that must be done.

I'm thinking of You, Jesus, when You mourned for the city of Jerusalem. You wept as You opened Yourself up to its agony . . . and then You went into the city to teach, to preach, and to heal. You did something about the causes of suffering.

Why do I find this kind of mourning so difficult, Lord? I'm learning to give myself up to a personal loss or tragedy, but this is something else. It's not always enough for me to feel someone else's pain, is it? And I can't express it simply in words or the touch of a hand. Much more is needed. In fact, this kind of mourning is very expensive — it means I must act. I must go to Jerusalem.

Perhaps, sensing the cost, I unconsciously try to shield myself. I turn away from this "Jerusalem" kind of mourning. Yes, a lot of us do. But You understand, Jesus . . . and You find ways to jolt us out of our apathy and bring us up close to our suffering, hurting, fellow human beings.

I'm remembering when our family first moved to La Jolla and we became interested in a project our church was involved in just across the border in Mexico. Along with several other churches and civic groups, we were helping to maintain a day school and maternity clinic in an impoverished area. Louie and I wanted to see how the project was coming along, so we asked the young minister in charge of it if our family could tag along on his next trip across the border. He agreed, and one beautiful, sunny Saturday morning the six of us piled into our car and followed our friend south for forty-five minutes. We were in another world.

We drove around a town bustling with tourists and shoppers and made our way to the hills and canyons. There, surrounded by hundreds of tiny shacks made of packing crates, scraps of tin, and cardboard boxes, was the *Casa* — day school, maternity clinic, and chapel, all in one small area.

I had spent summers in work camps, I had seen the aftermath of war . . . I was no stranger to deprivation at home and overseas. But I was not prepared for what I saw in those grim hills. This was *poverty* — and I will never use the word casually again.

I hope I'll always remember that day in my life. It's hard to believe that hope can rise from such depression, yet it did. Hope came in the form of the people who kept the *Casa* going . . . the lovely old Mexican lady who first saw the need for help many years ago and whose very presence is an inspiration to the staff . . . the Mexican teacher who runs the school . . . the American doctor who works there one day a week on her own time . . . and the volunteers who prepare and serve the children the only food most of them will eat all day. Truly, they are doers of the Word.

Children are quick to make friends, and as our four played with the *Casa* schoolchildren we talked as well as we could with the staff. There was a language barrier because none of us spoke fluent Spanish and the Mexicans spoke very little English, but we found that our hands and eyes could say a lot for us.

It was a long quiet drive home that evening. No one — not even Jamie, our youngest and liveliest — had much to say. When we arrived at our home (which suddenly looked very grand) we each went our own way, lost in our private thoughts. There was little sleep for any of us that night. We were in mourning.

We woke up feeling restless. We had wept for Jerusalem and now we wanted to do something — personally — about the misery we had seen there. But what?

Dan, our oldest son, was about eleven when we took our first trip to the *Casa*. Thoughtful, frugal with words, he didn't say much about how he felt. But at Christmastime that year, something he did told us very clearly. The students in his school decided not to exchange gifts with each other. Instead they sent food and toys to the *Casa*. The idea was Dan's, as we learned later from his principal. As head of the student council he had suggested the plan at a meeting, and when it was approved he helped organize it. Our son went to Jerusalem.

A few years later, during Easter vacation, Dan visited the *Casa* again. This time he went with a lot of his friends from church and they spent their vacation painting and repairing the school. It was a rewarding time for all of them.

Dan's ability to mourn, to feel another person's sorrow, has become an important part of his life. More and more we see it shaping him, leading him in ways that are right for him. Last summer he was part of an interracial team of American college students who went overseas to share Christian ways and means of meeting problems in depressed areas. It was more than an opportunity for them to serve — it was a meeting of minds, an exchange of ideas among young people from totally different backgrounds.

We're not all like Dan. Some of us take different roads to Jerusalem. And some of us turn back. It all depends upon our ability to sense sorrow and injustice, and our will to do something about them.

For some reason it helps me to experience sorrow directly or to know someone personally who is being mistreated — then I am stirred into action. It's just the way I am . . . the road I have to take.

One day several years ago I had a call from the mother of one of Jamie's classmates. Her name was Amy. She told me that the third grade, an unusually large class, was desperate for a room mother. Amy had been asked to help out and she said she would if another mother would share the load. I knew what was coming — would I be that other mother?

Well, I had just decided that my basket was full enough for the coming year. So I took a deep breath and explained how busy I was with children going to different schools, my church work and a few community activities. I saved the clincher for last: "You see, we have *four* children."

"Yes, I know," she said. "We have seven."

Well, I became Amy's helper for the year. We gave class parties and organized the usual activities during the holidays . . . and it was fun! We were a good team, and I made a wonderful new friend. Amy was a warm, open, considerate woman with a delightful sense of humor. We understood each other and could share the way we felt about our faith, our families, and the plain joy of being alive. It was a treat for us to be together. One night we even succeeded in getting our busy husbands to take us to a football game.

A few months ago something happened to change my relationship with Amy—and my life as well. I had a dream one night, and I, who can rarely remember my dreams, can still *feel* this one. In my dream I became Amy, and her children were mine. We were living in tiny rooms so crowded and cluttered that I felt I was losing my sense of dignity as a human being.

I woke up the next morning, a Sunday, feeling uneasy, angry, almost ill. I knew I had to find Amy, and when I went to church she was there, looking for me. For the first time since I had known her, the smile was gone from her face and her eyes were filled with tears. Would we be home that afternoon? She needed to talk.

We talked. And that afternoon Louie and I discovered another woman beneath Amy's cheerful, bouncy exterior. For Amy is black, and that day she told us what her life was really like—overworked, underpaid, she and her husband and children jammed into a four-room apartment because that was all they could afford.

This is important—Amy wasn't bitter. She didn't feel sorry

for herself. She didn't think the world owed her anything. But she was a woman, a wife, a mother, and she was hurting for her family. Oh, how she was hurting!

Knowing Amy, loving her as a friend, we hurt with her. We mourned . . . and we desperately wanted to help. How?

Somewhere in my memory something was calling for attention. What was it? A project—something our church mission commission was doing a few years ago . . . something that had caught my mind and interest, but not my heart.

I remembered! As I listened to Amy that Sunday and saw the pain in her eyes, I remembered that our mission commission had talked about sponsoring a low-income housing project for minority groups. A study had convinced them that this was our community's most urgent need. I knew the project was still in the works, but my passive support had not been enough to keep me informed of where it was at the moment.

Now it was different. I had a personal stake in that housing development because I was learning what it was like to live without it. And I knew what it would mean to someone I loved. Multiply that feeling by the number of families who could live in those new houses and you have a project that finally gets under way. Somehow two churches got together. Somehow two official boards joined forces under a determined and dedicated black pastor and our minister of missions. Somehow our congregations began to feel what I had felt . . . *human need*—not somebody else's need, but our own, for we were all one. A few weeks ago I looked at an architect's drawing of the project. Here and there in the split-level buildings the architect had sketched little stick figures representing men and women. But that wasn't what I really saw. No. I saw my friend Amy and her wonderful family comfortably settled in one of the larger apartments. And through seeing them, I saw their neighbors . . . *my* neighbors.

Thank You, Lord, for Amy . . . and for all the other Amys You will put in my life. I need them so. I want to be able to mourn, not only for myself but for others, just as You did. I want to be able to sense human need, and with Your help to find a way to meet that need. But first I must be free . . . free to feel sorrow. I'm not afraid of it anymore, for I too have seen the sun rise after the dark night. And it always will.

*Happy is the woman who honestly faces her loss and opens herself up to sorrow . . . in her life and in her world. Because she trusts God to come to her and heal her wounded spirit, she finds a new and deeper meaning in His presence. She knows that she will never be the same woman again, but she also knows that she is not alone. He is there in the loving gestures of the friends who walk close beside her. . . . He is there to guide her through life's darkest times. Her own strength is not enough to sustain her, but she knows now that she can lean on Him.*

# 3

Happy are those who claim nothing, for the whole earth will belong to them!

Matthew 5:5 PHILLIPS

Blessed are the meek: for they shall inherit the earth.

Matthew 5:5 KJV

# The Gentle Women

I have a problem with this Beatitude. Frankly, I've never cared for it. Usually I pass over it quickly and try to ignore it.

The word *meekness* bothers me . . . when I think of someone meek, I see a mousey, "Caspar Milquetoast" type of person, and I react. In fact, I react so strongly that when I come to the words "Gentle Jesus, meek and mild," I want to stop singing the hymn. That isn't the way I see Jesus . . . I see Him strong—gentle, yes, but certainly not meek.

Still, I can't accept all the other Beatitudes, with their revolutionary effects on my life, and pretend this one isn't there. Jesus apparently thought it was important . . . He included it among the most practical guidelines Christians have

43

ever been given. I must find out why . . . obviously I have
misunderstood it.

Perhaps the word *meekness* meant something different when
Jesus used it. I've never taken the time to learn the original
languages in which the Bible was written. I'll have to read
what scholars have to say. They can help me understand the
historical background . . . I need to sense the setting in which
the word was used. As I ask the Holy Spirit to teach me, He
often leads me to the work of a scholar—a scholar whose gift
opens up a whole new area of meaning to me.

I also look in the dictionary, but this time it doesn't help.
It appears we have no single word to describe what *meekness*
means in the biblical sense. And so I go to my Bible. As I
search its pages, some new meaning begins to appear. In the
Bible *meek* is used to describe two men—Moses and Jesus—
which says a lot in itself . . . neither of them could possibly
be considered *weak.* So what about meekness? What does it
mean? Ah, here it comes . . . a meek person doesn't fight or
argue with God. He doesn't defy His ways. No—just the opposite. A meek person submits his will to God. . . . He trusts
God to shape his will into a force for goodness . . . into something God can use.

As I pondered this deeper meaning, mumbling to myself,
my husband's curiosity was aroused. He pulled his Greek
New Testament from the shelf and read Matthew 5 aloud.
Then he checked it against his lexicon . . . and suddenly we
both became excited about the new ideas that became ap-
parent.

The Greek word for meek is *praos.* When used to describe
sound, it means "soft and gentle." When used to describe
an animal, it means "a wild animal that has been tamed"
. . . one no less strong, but one whose strength has been
channeled and made usable.

And when *praos* is used to describe a human being, it refers to a person who has been gentled, quieted, particularly after anger. This is not a weak person. This is a strong, spirited individual who has been tamed—molded—by God. He no longer flies off in all directions—he has a Way to go. Neither is his spirit broken . . . with God working through it, it is stronger than ever.

*Meekness,* then, means "strength" . . . but not raw power that may strike out and destroy. Meekness is gentle power . . . it builds, it lifts up, it restores.

The combination of gentleness with strength reminds me of two men we know who have similar qualities but use them in totally different ways. They both have talent, strong egos, and fascinating personalities, but that's where the similarity ends. One man lives for himself, driven by an ambition that can't seem to be satisfied. It isn't that he is cruel to his family, or that he doesn't care about them. I think he cares very much. It's just that he seems to be so driven—in his business as head of a large corporation, as well as in his social life among the VIP's who are always arriving, departing, overlapping. This man is also driven in his personal life . . . I get the feeling that he never wants to be alone, that perhaps he's afraid of solitude. But periodically his doctor puts him in the hospital for a few weeks, with a strictly enforced NO VISITORS sign on his door. And he is alone . . . but not by choice.

I don't know what drives our friend. It could be his desire for money, power, and position—or it could be some missing link in the chain of his life that makes him feel he has to prove something to be accepted by himself and the world. At any rate, I don't have to know why, because there is Someone who knows everything, absolutely everything, about our friend. He is the One—the only One—who can change his life patterns.

Louie and I love our friend very much . . . and in his way he tells us he loves us. We pray for him often . . . we pray that one day he will submit his life, with all its drivenness, to the One who knows and cares and can do something to help. We don't often put time limits on the Lord, but in this case, we pray that the miracle will happen before our friend's family is left bruised by the wayside . . . and before he is driven to destroy his own life.

The other man, equally aggressive and magnetic, has submitted his life to Christ . . . and what a difference that has made! Now, instead of using people, he allows God to use him as a blessing to so many lives.

He wasn't always that way. Louie and I met him before he knew Christ, and while he was an attractive person there was something reckless, almost destructive about him.

We met him at a party, one of the few that Louie and I have time to attend. I guess it's because I love people that I enjoy a good party. It's an adventure! There's always someone new to meet, someone whose life may be meant to touch mine, someone to be used by God to teach me something . . . and hopefully it works the other way around. That's why, before I go to a party, I always pray that I will be drawn toward the person God wants. And it has happened—many times.

It happened the night we met Hal. Just before we all sat down to dinner, there was a commotion at the door. It was a late and very noisy guest arriving. It was Hal. Obviously this wasn't his first party of the evening. Or perhaps he had had one all by himself before leaving home. Still, he was ready for conversation . . . in fact, he dominated it.

It was amazing how this man's presence seemed to fill the room. No doubt about it—here was a compelling, powerful personality. On the surface he was rough and loud, but as we were seated next to him for the rest of the evening, we began to see that the real man—the man underneath the scratchy surface—had great warmth, love, and sensitivity. We couldn't help thinking of the wonderful things God could do through such a man, if only . . . but Hal wasn't a Christian. He didn't seem to believe in anything but himself. Much as we coveted him for the Lord, we could only pray and wait.

Then, one Sunday a few weeks later, Hal and his whole family came to church—for the first time! I'm not sure why—perhaps out of curiosity . . . maybe a feeling of need. Anyway, it was just the beginning. In the months that followed, Hal stopped running his own life and turned it over to Christ.

Of course, I'm oversimplifying—it didn't happen that quickly. Nor did Hal give in easily. He struggled against submitting that powerful will to God—and at times he still struggles. From friends who knew him during his pre-Christian days, we learned that he was a man given to extremes. Some of this tendency remains—we see it cropping up every now and then—when he used to try to manipulate people into experiencing their faith in "the right way" (*his* way) . . . when he tried to link faith in Christ with a narrow political position. But always, because he is sincere in his commitment to Christ and puts Him before his own interests, he has abandoned these tactics. He has allowed himself to be led to where Christ is central to everything else in life. It's almost as if God had whispered to him, "You may be extreme in your love for Me, and in your love for your brothers and sisters in life, but nowhere else!"

Yes, Hal still struggles—but Jesus is a better, stronger, more persistent fighter! Now the real Hal has come to the surface where everyone can see him. He's a wonderful worker—not only in the church, but out in the community where his dynamic talents can do so much good. There seems to be no end to the things he can accomplish—but there is a difference in the way he uses his abilities. His strength—as great as ever—has been tamed. He uses it to lift up rather than to crush. Hal has gentle power.

Perhaps we must be strong before we can be gentle. It's

a matter of learning how to use our muscles, spiritual as well as physical . . . the hand that strikes learning to shield . . . the tongue that wounds learning words of comfort . . . seeking out a person's needs so that we may help instead of attack. . . .

Yes, I'm beginning to like this word *meekness.* And I wonder if it stretches the meaning too far to think of a meek person as someone bendable, adaptable to God and to life. Yes, I think it fits . . . and I think I need more meekness in my own life. So many things are changing today . . . our way of life, our values, our children, our institutions. I want to be able to shift gears easily . . . to understand and appreciate what is going on around me . . . to help wherever possible. So I can't be rigid. I must be bendable . . . strong enough on the inside to adapt on the outside. In other words, I must be meek in order to meet tomorrow.

*Adaptable* . . . that's a word I really like. *Happy are the adaptable* . . . it makes a lot of sense in our world. The unhappy people are the ones who feel threatened by the changes going on around them . . . they have little inner strength and so they look to traditions and institutions to give them a sense of security. Newness frightens them . . . they become rigid, and in their presence there is no peace.

But there are others who haven't hardened. Feeling the flow of life, they move in rhythm with it. Their trust in Christ is so real, and the security He gives them is so strong, that they cannot be threatened by change. They realize that newness is inherent in life . . . that if they themselves are going to expand and grow, they too must change. But they aren't dominated by change—they are free to evaluate it, to reject or accept it, according to its merits. These are the meek people of the world, and when I am with them I sense peace. With God's help, I want to be more like them.

Meek people don't make a lot of noise about their rights.

They will work for the rights of others, and in doing so they
secure rights for all. As Dr. Ralph Sockman stressed in *The
Higher Happiness,* the meek are more concerned with their
responsibilities . . . instead of grabbing, they offer. While
others fight their way through life, the meek walk quietly
with God.

Yes, these are the people who will inherit the earth . . . and
not by seizing it with force. The earth will come to them as a
gift, because they are the true children of God.

I certainly need to be adaptable. It's not only my world that
is changing . . . my home is, too—constantly. The only sure
thing about my schedule for any given day is that it will
change.

How many times I've started a day thinking, Ah, a quiet
one, at last!—only to end up with unexpected guests for lunch
or dinner, or a church group of fifty for a dessert meeting I
forgot to put on my calendar. At those times it helps to be
able to shift gears easily and noiselessly. (It also helps to have a
freezer full of goodies—especially when your teen-agers keep
the food situation in a constant state of emergency!)

Adaptability is something I've had to learn over the years,
and I think God has used the circumstances of my life to
make me more flexible. It wasn't easy for me during the early
years of our marriage. I wanted so much to please, but it was
hard for me to adjust to unexpected guests and interrupted
plans for the day. I was used to an ordered, methodical way
of life and suddenly my days were crowded with spontane-
ous activity. What a good thing it is that God created us with
a built-in ability to change.

When I married Louie, one of my friends said that I married into a family that crowds more into a week than most
families do in a year. And she was right . . . it was like jump-
ing onto a fast-moving train! It was fun, and how I loved my

new family — but sometimes I had to hold on for dear life!
The truth is, they had a lot to teach me about being adaptable — especially my mother-in-law, who to me will always be
the Queen of Adaptability.

Even during our student years, we didn't just go to school
— we also traveled for the seminary and worked with young
people. Later, studying in Scotland, we served a country
church part time. Now I can look back with gratitude for the
experience.

I remember when we took our first church full time and
found ourselves deeply involved in the lives of many people
. . . it was a whole new world of sharing, giving, and caring,
and I had never known such happiness. I had also never
known such busyness, either . . . the last shreds of my ordered, methodical existence were fraying rapidly. I could feel
myself becoming rigid, resisting the changes going on in
my life. Then I realized that *I* would also have to change. I
would be rigid and sink, or become flexible and learn to swim.
I couldn't change overnight — we human beings aren't made
that way. But I knew, too, that God would help me to adapt,
little by little. And of course He did.

Now interruptions are so much a part of my life that I can
hardly believe I ever resented them. Surprisingly, I have
found "swimming" stimulating and pleasant — so long as I
have a little raft in the sun where I can climb aboard and be
totally alone. I'm talking about the few moments I set aside
for myself every day, no matter how hectic life may be. This
is *my* time — my time for prayer, for books, for quietness, or
simply goofing off. It is the one ordered part of my life, and
when my own inner needs have been met, I find that I am
much more adaptable to the needs of the people around me.
It seems that in taming us, God makes us useful to the others
in our lives.

*Meekness* . . . it's beginning to sound better, stronger, now that I know more about it. And meekness is something I need every day . . . for I must be adaptable to far more than the changes that occur in my world. I must develop an attitude of meekness—of adaptability—to the people around me, especially my family.

Lately I've been thinking a lot about our children and about the way our relationship to each other will change more quickly in the years ahead. All four of them are teen-agers now, which means they are in a period of enormous growth and development. Their beings are emerging, taking shape . . . and I can see how totally different they are from one another. Each one is a unique person, and I must adapt to their individuality.

A little while ago I realized—quite suddenly—that our children were no longer children. We were on a long vacation in Barbados—actually it was a study sabbatical for my husband. We were staying in a house our good friends loaned to us . . . a wonderful old mill house on a remote part of the island. Life was quiet and simple . . . no radio and, of course, no TV . . . the nearest city was many miles away and we had no car to take us there. Nothing invaded our world except the sun, the sea, the wind, and the simple things we had to do to live. We had our books and each other . . . and we discovered that we were very rich.

And there, in the midst of such blessings, God opened my eyes and I saw my children in a new way. Louie saw it, too. It dawned on both of us one night after we all lingered a long time at the dinner table. The food (fish speared by our sons) had been good and the candles were burning low . . . but still we talked on and on . . . discussing, reminiscing, laughing. It was delightful, enjoying each other so much—and then I realized that our children were growing up. They weren't just "our children" . . . they were people, people I genuinely liked. I enjoyed their company, their humor, their way of thinking. They were my friends.

That means I must be sensitive to their uniqueness . . . aware of their changing needs. They'll be meeting new situations in life, new people . . . they will change. And so must I.

Now that our boys tower over me, now that our daughter borrows any of my clothes that happen to be up-to-date, I find myself asking, "What can I do for them?" When they were little they needed me in so many tangible, obvious ways —and how that fulfilled my need to be needed! Now they will need me less . . . and in different, more subtle ways. As Dr. Haim Ginott puts it, "Their need is to have you *not* need them." This will require meekness from me. As they need me less, I must find other areas of life where I am needed more.

Then, too, like most other mothers of the world, I've done my share of dreaming about the future of our four children. And yet, even though I keep my dreams to myself, I'm not sure it's good for parents to form specific ambitions for their children. That's forcing a goal on them in words they may not hear but will nevertheless sense—and they should have goals of their own.

I can't help but think of another mother who, like me, "treasured all these things in her heart" and no doubt had glorious dreams for her Son. Was meekness hard for her, too? Did she struggle when it was time for her to give up her dreams so that God's plans for her Son could be fulfilled? And did she finally realize—as I must—that being a parent means molding children into *themselves,* not into what we may need for ourselves? I think she did . . . and I pray that I will, too.

What can I *do* for my children? The answer is obvious and I must accept it. . . . I must be like a mother bird sitting quietly, patiently, on the branch of a tree, watching as her young ones try their own wings. No longer does she hover

over the nest, offering the fluttering protection of her wings.
That time is past. Now she preens her feathers with motherly
pride when the little ones take flight . . . perhaps she hurts
when they fall, yet she remains on the branch until they try
again, refusing to interfere with the process that will eventually make them strong and free. If there is real danger,
she is ready to go to them in an instant . . . and as there is always one whose need is greater than the others, she is ready
to answer when he calls. But she is also ready to sit . . . and
watch . . . and wait.                                              !

Dear Jesus, I'm not as patient as the mother bird, but it
helps me to think of her — her quiet strength, her respect for
her young, her meekness. That's what I need more of, Lord
. . . this meekness, this inner strength . . . this bending to
Your will. Then I'll be able to let my children learn to fly.

I can no longer ignore this Beatitude, Jesus. In fact, now
that I understand what meekness really is, I like it . . . and
I'm asking You to put more of it in my life. You know how
much I can use it.

*Happy is the woman who allows God to use her strength for
His own good purposes. This woman has gentle power . . . she
claims nothing for herself, but gives her life away in service to her
family, to her friends, to her community, and to all those whom God
has placed "in her basket." For by serving them, she is serving Christ.
Like her Master, she is truly meek — not weak — and as He served
others with no thought of anything in return, so does she. Yet love,
respect, an honored place in the world, a feeling of worth and useful-
ness — everything a woman craves — will be hers. What more could a
woman want from this world?*

# 4

Happy are those who are hungry and thirsty for
goodness, for they will be fully satisfied!

Matthew 5:6 PHILLIPS

Blessed are they which do hunger and thirst
after righteousness: for they shall be filled.

Matthew 5:6 KJV

# The Fulfilled Women

I have to dig deep into this Beatitude . . . at first it seems
obvious. . . . Don't we all want to be good? And don't we feel
much better when we do the right thing?

But there's more to these words than I see on the surface.
I've been influenced by my world and its conveniences. . . . If
I'm thirsty, I drink . . . if I'm hungry, I eat. Frankly, I don't
give these needs much thought, because they can be satisfied
so easily.

Suppose, though, that I lived in a desert land where water
was scarce and one crop failure could mean starvation? Ah,
yes, what about hunger and thirst under those conditions?
Now I begin to see a difference . . . hunger and thirst become driving, powerful, urgent needs. They motivate my life

and everything I do. I no longer simply *want* food and drink
— *I must have them!* Without them I can't survive. And underneath all our modern conveniences, this is still true.

It is true of the spirit, too—and that's really what Jesus is
telling us in this Beatitude. He's saying that it's not enough
simply to *want* goodness . . . we must *crave* it. This world is
our soul's desert . . . and unless our soul receives the quench-
ing, nourishing qualities of goodness, it will perish.

There are right things and wrong things in life, and most
of the time we can tell the difference between them. But just
doing the right things because we think we should leaves us
with an empty feeling. There's something wrong and we get
no satisfaction out of it.

Jesus promises that satisfaction will come to those who seek
the good things of God. He says that they will be filled—not
with the material goods of this world, not with an easy way
of life, not with something of limited value that can be taken
away from them . . . but with the joy and contentment that
come from doing God's will. The filled people are the truly
happy people in life.

I think our young people understand this . . . if that seems
like too much of a generalization, let's say that the young
people I'm close to understand it. They sense what it takes
to make life rich and full—they know it has little to do with
money, possessions, and power, and much to do with giving,
serving, and just plain enjoying. I admire their values. Our
four children, for instance, would rather spend a vacation
backpacking in the Sierra Nevada—which we've been doing
ever since they were old enough to weather the trip—than
at a fancy resort. (Which is fortunate for us, because we can't
afford a resort, anyway!)

If there is such a thing as a generation gap today, it's certainly being widened by a difference in values. So many of
our young people are disillusioned by their parents' obses-

sion with the things money can buy. While there are some families who seem to grow closer together with the years, there are others who are torn apart by what they seek. . . . Rebellious, disappointed children trying to pull down the expensive roof their parents put over their heads . . . parents giving their children everything — except themselves.

I'm reminded of Pam, a lovely girl and the only child of parents who gave her every physical blessing they could buy. The only thing Pam didn't have was a warm, loving relationship at home — and she needed that above all else. But closeness takes time, and Pam's parents were too busy making money to give her time. Closeness means a commitment, too, but that had already been given to a corporation. We saw what was happening, but there was no way to communicate our concern . . . where there is a difference in values, there is also a difference in language. So it was no surprise when our phone rang late one night and we learned that Pam had run away.

I wish there could be a happy ending to this story, but there just isn't. Pam's parents know where she is, but they still can't reach her "where she lives." Fortunately for Pam, she's young, so we can still hope that she'll find happiness in her life . . . but I don't think she'll go looking for it among "things."

Lord, I'm so glad You didn't say, "Happy are those who *are* good. . . ." Who could possibly claim that! Not I! But You said, *Happy are those who hunger and thirst* after *goodness* . . . . Quite a different thing!

There have been times when I have hungered and thirsted for more of You in my life, Jesus . . . and as I look back over the years I can see that these have been the best moments. But there have been other times when I've been caught up in silly things . . . things that had no real meaning . . . and they left me with an empty heart. And so the practical truth of this Beatitude is becoming very clear to me. . . . Our happiest moments *are* those spent in seeking You and following Your Way in life.

But how do we do that, Lord? We're such material beings, and we live in a world that is built to serve our material desires. And yet it's only when we live the life of the spirit that we can find peace.

I guess we've got our work cut out for us . . . we have to turn our attention away from goods and toward goodness. I suppose we can begin in our minds . . . by thinking of goodness. . . . That's fine — but You know how imaginations are . . . the world is full of distractions, and our imaginations can run wild, leaving all our intentions far behind.

No . . . I'm sure there's a better way. . . . In Romans 12 it says, "Don't let the world around you squeeze you into its own mold, but let God remold your minds from within. . . ." Yes, God can do the job so much better than we can. If we let Him into our minds He can transform our imaginations. Then we can think in His terms.

We do have spiritual desires, just as we have material ones, but they need cultivation . . . deep inside us they hunger and thirst for the food they need to keep our inner beings alive. We have to bring these desires to the surface of our lives where they can influence what we do. And gradually our appetites will change. . . . "Taste and see that the Lord is good . . ." (Psalms 34:8 KJV). Yes, He is *very* good, and once we have tasted the kind of satisfaction that comes from following Him, we'll want more.

It seems to me that what we seek has a lot to do with who we really are. In other words, we become *like* the things we want most in life. And if it's money we want, we'll find a way to get it . . . but it will also get us.

That happened to a friend of mine. From the time we were

teen-agers, she knew exactly what she wanted out of life—
money and security—and plenty of both. Because she was a
girl of high moral standards, I knew she wouldn't com-
promise them to reach her goal. But she was also very determined and I never doubted that she would get what she
wanted. Yes, she did . . . she made it to the top on her own
and on her enormous talent. Then she married a very wealthy
man. She had everything she wanted . . . or so it seemed. But
strange things began to happen to her life. . . . It was no
longer her own. Her days were crowded with meetings,
managers, contracts, and endless red tape. Boards were
formed to handle her money.

Our friend was a warm, caring woman who loved her
family, but she found less and less time for it. She belonged
to her possessions and she was becoming like one of them.
When she finally realized it, she began to fight for her freedom. With the honesty that was typical of her she began to
search her spirit, listening for the voice of need. And the
voice was very faint, because her spirit had gone unfed for a
long time.

My friend made changes in her life . . . it took time and it
took courage . . . most of all it took faith—faith in the
promise that she could have a filled, satisfied life. First of all,
she began saying *no* to the things in her life . . . she didn't
*have* to spend all her time making money . . . she didn't *have*
to worry about security . . . she even considered the worst
things that might happen if she lost everything. *Everything?*
Well, she found she could live without the things she owned,
but not without the people she loved. As long as she had her
husband and children, she was rich . . . none of her possessions had any real value . . . and once she was willing to let
go of them, they had no hold on her.

Jesus' promise was kept, as it always is. As my friend's
appetites changed (and appetite is what this Beatitude is all

about), her life began to fill with happiness. Her days were spent with the people she loved and her greatest joy came from the things they did together. She's still a very rich woman, but she has learned, as Christians should, to wear her possessions loosely. She uses them to bless others, as she has been blessed. Amazingly, they have blessed her, too—they have brought her close to human need, and this is what she hungers and thirsts to ease. Yes, in many, many ways my friend is deeply satisfied . . . at last.

I had another friend who sought fame. Somehow she felt that if she could make it big in her field she would have everything she could ever want. She was so lovely, so talented, so filled with potential as a human being . . . and she traded it all for a promise that never came true. She made it to the top, all right, and she had more fame than she could handle . . . but her spirit went hungry. At the peak of her career she was a lonely, dejected, disillusioned woman trying to find warmth in a cold, materialistic world. . . . And so she kept climbing higher, reaching out—but for what? She never seemed to know, and neither did any of us who loved her. We were aware of her loneliness, her spiritual and very human need, and we tried in our fumbling ways to help, but she always seemed just beyond our reach. If only she had been able to put her inner needs first . . . but her life ended, much too soon. I know it may seem odd to say that she died from a kind of starvation of the spirit—but I honestly believe she did.

There are some things in life we cannot understand, and this is one of them for me. I simply have to give it to God and go on. But whenever I remember my friend—and I often do—I pray that God will use me in the lives of the women I know. I'm not clever or witty or full of special wisdom . . . but one thing I know, both from my own experience and from those who are close to me: Happiness doesn't come from money or fame or achievement . . . it comes from God. And the closer we get to Him, the greater our joy will be.

Today we hear a lot about the importance of being fulfilled as a woman. I couldn't agree more . . . and this Beatitude shows us the way — *Happy are the women who hunger and thirst after goodness . . . they shall be filled.*

Perhaps we may have different ideas about what fulfillment is . . . some of us want to put special talents to work . . . some want to right wrongs . . . some want to call attention to injustices . . . some want to add beauty to the world . . . some want to preserve it. There are so many worthy causes calling out to us.

I'm all for the gals who can do these things, but not all of us can be protestors . . . or crusaders . . . or teachers . . . or artists. Not all of us can juggle a home and a career without fumbling. Many of us will seek fulfillment right where we are . . . and that's usually at home.

When I think of being fulfilled as a woman, I think of being needed . . . the two, at least to me, are inseparable. Years ago, when we were studying in Scotland and our children were small, our life was simple. We shared an old, large house with another student family (later our very good friends), and we each paid twenty-seven dollars rent a month. Our basement kitchen had no modern conveniences. No refrigerator — but in Scotland, who needs one! No fancy stove — but a reliable old one we picked up at an auction. No central heating — but wonderful fireplaces. No washing machines — and with two babies in diapers, I could have used one, even in Scotland! There was lots of work, lots of joy, and lots of feeling very needed. Yes, I was fulfilled every minute of every day, and it was deeply satisfying.

Later, back home in the States, I had all the helpful gadgets, and the work load was different. But I still felt needed. Our children's needs were more intangible, but just as real. . . .

Sometimes, as mothers, we begin to feel left out and a little obsolete when our children are no longer physically dependent upon us. . . . Perhaps this is when we should let our hearts feel out their needs . . . the need for us to be there when they come home from school . . . to listen when they're hurting . . . to hold them (if they're still small enough) . . . to rub a back when they're down and don't know why. This feeling, listening, scratching, rubbing — just being there — may be the world's most intangible ministry, but it's certainly the most filling. And its fullness will last us a lifetime.

It's a funny thing about seeking God's good things for yourself and your family . . . you find that you want them for others, too.

I remember that when I was a new Christian, I was eager to share my faith with everyone . . . the new life I had found was just too wonderful to keep to myself — and I certainly didn't . . . it overflowed onto everyone I met. As I look back I can see that I had more enthusiasm than tact. I remember one evening when I was having dinner with an actor friend and telling him about all the good things God had done for me — for everyone — for *him*. I'm afraid I never even stopped for breath. Finally, in desperation, he interrupted me and said, "Hold it — I believe! I believe!"

For a long time I had hungered and thirsted after God and His Way . . . and when He came into my life I felt such joy, such love and peace, such an awareness of life . . . it was so beautiful that I wanted everyone to know Jesus, my Liberator. I still do. . . .

But seeking after God and His goodness isn't limited to our spiritual lives. There are things to be done on earth . . . in our world. If I seek a good life and social justice for myself and my family, I must see that others have it, too. I must be-

come involved in the world outside my door. How much involvement depends upon the other demands on my time.
. . . One year I may work with a group that is trying to lift
the level of life in the ghetto . . . another year I may work
toward the passage of a bill that I feel is needed in a ne-
glected area of our society. . . . In other years I hope to do
more.

There is work to be done close to home, among our friends
and neighbors, as we share life together. Last year, two of
our teen-agers wanted to go to a Young Life Summer Camp.
These camps are not only the most fun, but the most effec-
tive ones we know for high-schoolers, so Louie and I were
glad to eke the money out of our budget. Then we discovered
that two of our boys' friends wanted to go, and one of them
clearly couldn't afford it. As I was thinking and praying about
our problem, I got a call from some Young Life workers in
our city. They were trying to raise funds for scholarships
to their summer camps . . . and would I help out by speaking
to a women's group? *Would* I!

Public speaking isn't my thing—in fact, I don't particularly
enjoy it. But when I'm enthusiastic about something I'm willing to try. So try I did, and at that morning get-together we
raised enough money to provide several young people with
camp scholarships. And yes, our young friend got one of
them. What's more, while he was at camp he became convinced that God loved him . . . his response was so full and
natural that his life became a whole new ball game. . . . Now,
*that's* satisfaction!

A woman's life has seasons, and I'm about to enter a new one.
Our older sons are away at college, and the other two children
are following close behind. In a few years our house will be a
much quieter place. I'll have to be adaptable, for I'll be
needed in different ways. With four children in college at the

same time, I may be needed to help provide bread for our table, and I may find myself working outside our home for the first time in twenty years. . . .

And when the children are educated and on their own — what then? Ah, what then? Which of our dreams will we turn to? So many times over the years Louie has said, "When the children are grown, let's. . . ." So it's not a question of "What then?" but "Which one?" Which new thing? Which ministry of faith? Which adventurous service? For when your children are grown and no longer need you the same way they once did, there is always a world full of need outside your door.

Needs . . . needs . . . that's what this Beatitude is all about . . . our own needs and those of others . . . reaching out toward each other to share our love and faith. Yes, we need each other . . . our spirits hunger and thirst to make contact with each other . . . to touch each other's lives, just as Jesus did. This is living in the spirit. This is hungering and thirsting after goodness.

God has a place and a task for us, no matter what our season of life. You and I will always be needed . . . somewhere — by someone — and *that* is our fulfillment.

*Happy is the woman whose heart yearns for the deep things of God. . . . This woman seeks for spiritual riches rather than the things of this world . . . she knows that there are others with needs greater than her own, and she is not satisfied simply to look after her own family's well-being. Her love and faith reach out to those around her, and through her God is able to touch the lives of many persons. The happiness she knows will be deeper and greater and more lasting than anything this world can offer her.*

# 5

Happy are the merciful, for they will have mercy
shown to them!

Matthew 5:7 PHILLIPS

Blessed are the merciful: for they shall obtain
mercy.

Matthew 5:7 KJV

# The Generous Women

The simple, direct words of our Lord have a way of digging
into my complacent life and stirring things around. Like
leaven in a loaf, they will make me stretch and grow. It's
not an altogether comfortable experience—change rarely
is. Shall I come back to the Beatitudes another time? Find
something else to do? There are so many things. . . . No.
Without change, there can be no growth. So it must be.

Right away I run into trouble. I'm not sure what *mercy* is.
Or how it works. Or what it will do to my life. Mercy can
mean kindness—compassion—forbearance. . . . But the word
is hardly used anymore and my mind keeps tripping over it.
It's too dramatic, too big, for everyday life and seems to belong to a crisis—". . . God, have mercy on a sinner like me"

(Luke 18:13). Yes, it belongs there. *Mercy* is a God-sized word.

Perhaps another word, another translation, will help. Yes, here it is: *generous*. That's a person-sized word. *Happy are those who are generous with others. . . . God will be generous with them.*

All right, then, what about generosity? As I turn the word over in my mind I immediately think of giving — giving things, money, time. "Happy birthday, dear!" "It's just what I wanted!" "Sure, I'll help out." "We gave at the office."

And yet, something tells me that Jesus was talking about a deeper, more demanding kind of generosity. What else can I give? My hands, my mind, my attention, my love, my understanding? Even more? *Happy are those who give lavishly of themselves. . . .* Yes, I think that's what Jesus meant.

Suddenly my thoughts race back through the years. . . . My husband and I were very young and everything was new. Life seemed to come rushing at us all at once and we met it eagerly, head-on. Lou was in his first church, and the congregation was new, too. The sanctuary wasn't built yet, so having nowhere else to go we held our meetings in our home — two of the weeklies were men's prayer breakfasts at 7:00 A.M.! People were constantly stopping by with ideas, concerns, problems. And then there was the phone, always the phone. It would be understating the situation to say that my plate was full, and so was my house! As a minister's wife there was much for me to do, and I was also the mother of four children, all of them under the age of five. I loved my life, but it was wearing me out. I was hungry for rest and quiet, and there was none in sight.

Worst of all, I was starved for my husband. Longingly I recalled our student days in Edinburgh when we used to walk for miles — talking, moving fast to brace ourselves against the chill wind blowing in from the North Sea. We had been so close then, but now I practically had to wave to him from across the room. I was proud of Lou and the work he was doing. I was glad to share him with our family, our congregation—with the whole world, if necessary. But I needed him too!

It's never wise to hold your feelings in. They have a way of bursting into the open when you least expect it. That's what happened to me. I should have told my husband then how I felt, but I didn't want to burden him with my problems when he already was carrying so many others that were bigger. And so I kept quiet—until one night when we were getting dressed for the evening services.

Lou had come home very excited about a new project. Ordinarily I loved listening to his plans, his hopes, and his dreams, but that night my own frustration began to well up inside me. As he went on enthusiastically I could hear our front door opening and closing as the early birds began to arrive. I knew I had to speak, to tell my husband how much I needed him. *Right now?* something inside me said, disapprovingly. *Yes, now!* I thought, but instead of words, my tears came. (I don't cry often, but at the right moment it seems to work wonders!) Again I tried to speak and although I don't remember much of what I said, my husband apparently got the message. I was hungry for him!

It was Lou's response that made me remember that night years later, for he was truly generous. He waited until my tears stopped and he listened to me, which wasn't easy to do with one hundred people sitting in our front room waiting for the service to begin. Then he was generous in his attitude as he shared my need, saying he needed me too. He was generous in his action as he promised, with God's help, to give me my time—no, to make sure we had *our* time together. And through the years, he has been generous in his determination to keep that promise. In spite of his hectic schedule, and often against enormous odds, he has kept our special times and our short trips away together as something sacred that must not be violated.

Many times I have heard my husband turn down invitations to meetings, speaking engagements, and almost anything that happens to fall on our night. "No, I'm sorry," he'll say, "but I have an important appointment for that night and I want to keep it." And with those words he tells me "I love you" better than all the flowers and heart-shaped boxes of candy in the world. He knows I don't want things—I want him. And he wants me.

You really don't have to go far to get away. There are hundreds of glamorous places in the world and hundreds of exciting ads telling you how to get there and how much fun you'll have. Travel is a treat and I love it, but it's expensive. Sometimes a man and wife simply need *to be*—and *to be* together. How often we forget about that because we put other, more material goals first in our lives. It's normal, I suppose, for a wife to want to help her husband get ahead, to make his dreams come true, but what good is worldly success if a man and his wife are strangers by the time they achieve it? Maybe a wife can do more than support a husband's ambitions. Maybe she can remind him that their life needs its quiet moments away from the pressures of work and even those of family. Stillness, when it is shared with someone you love, can be a very rich experience.

I'm grateful for the many moments of stillness Louie and I have known together. Believe me, it wasn't always easy to arrange them during our busy life, and there were times when we thought it would be simpler to forget the whole idea. But we didn't, and I hope we never will.

Sometimes we were so broke that after we paid a baby-sitter to come in for the evening we didn't have a cent left to spend on ourselves. But we didn't mind. We went for long, long walks in the lovely hills where our first church was being built.

Now we walk the beaches of La Jolla, often between midnight and dawn if there seems to be no other time we can call ours. Sometimes we talk, eagerly pouring out all the feelings that have waited to be expressed. Sometimes we don't say a word — and that's all right, too.

Getting away on short trips together has taken real ingenuity, especially when the children were small. With a little luck we could "child swap." That meant we would take care of our neighbors' children while their parents went off together for a weekend — and then a few weeks later they would return the favor. Having sleeping bags and bodies all over the house was a treat for our children, and for me it was easier than squeezing money from our budget for a baby-sitter.

Recently some friends came up with a wonderful offer. They have a guest house and simply gave us the key to it. Now, when we put aside a day and a night — or even part of a day — for ourselves, we arrange for someone to look after the children, pack a bag, hop in the car, and drive four blocks to "the little house below." It's quiet, convenient — and free!

The time we take for ourselves may seem like a little thing, but I think it makes the difference between our being turned on or turned off to each other. It has helped to make our marriage a daily happening instead of a situation that exists. In giving us the time and the opportunity to be generous, it has blessed us with great happiness. (Thank you, Louie, for hearing me out that night. . . .)

I wonder, though — have I always responded to my husband's needs as generously as he has to mine? I'm thinking of the times when he comes home unexpectedly for a half hour between counseling appointments, after a funeral, before a wedding. Sometimes I can sense that he wants me to stop whatever I'm doing and sit down and listen to him, or perhaps just be with him. Whenever I do, I'm glad. But very often I don't. Very often I'm too busy *doing* something to take time out to *be* someone to my husband. Those are the times I am not generous with myself. Generous with my services, yes, but not with *me,* and at that moment my husband couldn't care less about my talents as a homemaker. He needs me as a friend, as a woman, as a lover—yet he has to play second fiddle to a vacuum cleaner.

Like most women I like a clean house, but sometimes I think there can be too much housework and not enough home. We've all heard wives of late-working husbands say, "I don't want his money—I want *him.*" Yet, I wonder how many husbands would like to say, "Forget the house—I want a wife."

I admit I have a problem with neatness. I think it comes from being an only child and being brought up by my mother and grandfather. Affluent we were not, but we were very clean and neat, which is not so difficult with only three in the family. I grew up with a built-in sense of order, which is rather pleasant to live with when you're all by yourself. But when you're part of a large, busy family, when your daughter sews and enjoys crafts, when your three sons make surf boards in the garage and model airplanes in the attic, when your husband is a gifted do-it-yourselfer whose work doesn't allow him time to finish his projects on schedule—an overdeveloped sense of order can be a real drag.

My family is very generous with my passion for neatness, yet I know it bugs them. I'm trying to learn how to be more casual, but sometimes Lou has to take me by the hand and lead me away from a cluttered kitchen or an unfolded pile of laundry. "That can wait," he'll say. "This is our chance to do something as a family." He's right, and he's a good teacher.

Frankly, it bothers me to leave the dishes in the sink, and I don't like to see my husband run out of clean socks. But when my family says "Let's go," I have learned to ask myself,

"What's the worst thing that can possibly happen if I don't clean the kitchen?" Leaving my work undone has never lost me a friend or caused the sky to fall in or the world to come apart. It has enabled me to give myself to the people I love.

In exchange for a little dust on the tabletops, I now have a much bigger world to live in. I am part sailor, hiker, camper, researcher, painter, swimmer, flashlight holder, photographer, driver, skirt measurer, and critic-at-large. I can lend a hand, a foot, a shoulder, or an ear to many things that did not exist for me a few years ago. What's more important, I feel I am woman, wife, mother, friend, companion, confidante, and occasional umpire. That's about all I can handle.

Now I'm beginning to understand why Jesus urged us to be lavish in our giving. It's because generosity is a magical quality that seems to increase as it is used. I'm pretty convinced that nervous breakdowns don't come from overwork (or overgiving), but from worrying about all the work or keeping track of all the giving.

I find that the more I am able to give myself to my family, the more I have to give. I do not wear out. I am not used up.

Neither am I diminished as a person. I don't feel I am an appendage of my husband or my children. In giving of myself I am finding out who I am—and there is more to me than I thought! I am part of my husband, and for a season I am part of my children. I am an influence in their lives. They need me. They need what I am and what I have to give. And in responding to those needs I am discovering myself.

Again, it's a matter of words and what they mean to us. If I think of a need as a demand, I'm going to resent it and pull away. But if I think of a need as an open-armed invitation to share the love and life of someone dear to me, I can only be grateful it came my way.

When a woman is married she has a special and very beautiful opportunity to make generosity meaningful in a physical sense. I'm not talking about the sharing of tasks in a home, important as these are. No, right now I'm thinking about a man and woman who are very much in love, whose lives are joined in the sight of God, and who freely give their bodies in a joyous ministry to each other.

These days we hear so much about sex *before* marriage and *outside* marriage, that you'd think sex is exciting only when it's illicit. The momentary tingle, the tang of guilt, the sudden splurge of passion—these are all we hear about sex. But there is so much more and it is so much better.

Sex doesn't make the marriage, but it can certainly break it. Some marriages, too many marriages, suffer from an incomplete sex life. But that isn't the way married sex *has* to be. It's not at all what it *can* be. There are other kinds of marriages, marriages that constantly grow in honesty, friendship, goal sharing, love, and the physical expression of that love. These marriages have soul!

Sex not only gives life; it celebrates the life God gave each of us. It is a powerful force that can become terribly destructive if it is cut off from its natural environment, love. Then it can become unprincipled, fickle, selfish, hateful, even violent, almost as if it wants to destroy the life it was meant to serve. This is the kind of sex we read so much about.

Only in a marriage—a marriage where love is—can sex develop into the delightfully positive force God meant it to be. Here is where the excitement of sex really is. When a man and a woman make a lifelong commitment to love and cherish each other, they are giving themselves the time they will need to dismantle the barriers of restraint, shyness, defensiveness, and selfishness that exist between all human beings. It cannot be done in a night or with a rush of passion. It takes time to know and be known.

In a marriage a man and a woman can discover the thrill of trusting each other so fully that their freedom of expression reaches undreamed-of heights. Their intimacy becomes a sanctuary, a place where the soul of their relationship can grow through their physical oneness. No matter how many others they may share life with in the circle of family and responsibilities, they have a small private world where they can offer each other their trust, their vulnerability, and the unrestrained affirmation of their love.

Generosity in the physical relationship of marriage brings each partner great dividends. In giving of themselves they also receive in kind, and this reciprocity of love is beautiful beyond words. A marriage with a good healthy sex life can also weather all kinds of pressures from the outside.

It sounds very stern to urge Christian wives to submit themselves to their husbands (Ephesians 5:22). Here again it's a matter of words and what they mean. How much better it is to think of *submitting* as *giving*. And how much better it is to think of sex as an opportunity to give our love to our husbands in every possible way—emotionally, physically, mentally. Perhaps this is the way to achieve a truly spiritual expression of love.

Yes, generosity enlarges my life and brings me closer to my family. But there is a world outside my front door, and I live there too. It needs a part of me, just as my family does—and I need it!

My mind turns to the national and international scene. I wonder what would happen between nations, between races, between just plain human beings if the generosity of Jesus were applied to all our relationships. It wouldn't be easy, because when Jesus gives, He gives totally, with no strings attached. Could we Americans, for example, give aid to an emerging nation and resist the desire to tell its people how to live their lives? Could we really put their interests ahead of our own if we had to make that decision? If we could, and if people all over the world became convinced that we wanted everyone to reach his full potential as a human being, how different the human and the international scenes might be.

Right here in our own country there are so many ways we could be more generous with each other. We mean well, but sometimes we don't give well — or enough. If only we could go beyond the giving of our resources and time. If, for instance, we could help our black brothers achieve the goals they set for themselves instead of offering them our goals, we would be on our way to becoming one nation under God.

I'm thinking of a lesson I learned a couple of years ago while doing some volunteer work on one of our city's ghetto programs. Yes, like most other cities, we have a ghetto, and like most other cities we're trying to do something about it. The program I was working with was a truly happy experience for everyone involved in it. It was successful, I feel, because it was a program *for* black people, *headed* by black people and *run* by black people. I and others like me helped in small, practical ways — such as sitting on a board — but only when needed and asked. It cost us very little in terms of time and money, but we did have to give something of ourselves. We had to give way.

When I really open my eyes to what is going on around me I see that the spirit of generosity is growing . . . in the young people of our church who gave up their Easter vacation to go to Mexico where they and the local young people rebuilt a school; in some of my busy neighbors with large families of their own who somehow squeeze out a few hours each week to tutor children in depressed areas. I almost gasp when I visualize the potential for generosity among our retired citizens.

It's strange, isn't it, how life becomes stale and meaningless when we think we have nothing left to give? So it was with some of the older people in our community. But then the rest of us realized that we were wrong and so were they — their lives were far from finished. Our city needs them more than ever and they need the challenge service offers. "Give us of yourselves," we said. "Give us of your experience, your wisdom, your love for mankind. This is your great opportunity to serve."

Some of these people thought they were beyond the age of involvements. The brightness had gone from their eyes and they were sitting back, resigning themselves to a dreary, monotonous future. But now they're alive again because they're being used creatively in a whole new revolution.

I see retired schoolteachers tutoring minority children on a one-to-one basis in the tutorial program held in our church. I see retired businessmen sharing their years of experience with men who want to start businesses of their own. I see retired builders, land investment developers, and lawyers working on low-income housing projects in all areas of our city — one of them sponsored by our church. Yes, the potential amount of generosity coming into the world is staggering, and I am caught up in the wonder of such thoughts . . . until some minor crisis with one of my children brings me back, back to the world where I live.

All right, I'm in my own backyard once more and I see I still have *much* to learn about giving. I have friends, neighbors; new people will be coming into my life. What can I give them? What do they need from me?

Perhaps the most generous thing I can do is to let them be whatever they are. In other words, I must not judge them. When my neighbor's political views turn out to be just the opposite of mine, I must not resent her. Not that we can't differ openly and honestly, but I must not try to change her into something I want her to be. If I am to be generous about our differences, I must respect my neighbor's ideas, much as I might dislike them. Somehow I don't think Jesus wanted us to manipulate each other.

Neither must I judge people by outward appearance. How a person speaks or looks, what he wears or doesn't wear, has nothing to do with what he is. This seems to be especially true of our young people today. As one song goes, "Look past the hair and into the eyes. . . ."

Some years ago my husband and I learned how important it is to take that second look. We went to a dinner party where all the other guests were either students or young people employed by the university near us. In fact, we were the only over-thirty people there, and we felt like real squares.

The moment we entered the room I felt my old habit take over. In one quick glance I had sized up everyone, or so I thought. And believe me, there was a lot to glance at—beards, long hair, bare feet, strange clothes. We have two boys in college now and they have really helped their mom reach the point where I don't even see these things anymore—but at that time I felt uncomfortable because I didn't seem to fit in.

Well, as the evening went on and the conversation became open and honest, we all discovered that our differences were quite superficial. One by one the barriers of age, dress, and life-style broke down and we took a second look at each other. We were very much alike. Beneath some rather alarming exteriors our fellow guests were warm, sensitive, concerned human beings who were very generous about accepting the two squares in their midst. My split-second glance on coming into the room had been all wrong. I realized, for instance, that the biggest hang-up didn't belong to the boy with the longest hair or the girl with the shortest mini. It belonged to me.

Friendships began that night as we shared our similar joys and concerns. We found we had our differences, too, but we were able to talk about them honestly. We were learning to give each other the right to be ourselves.

I can see now that generosity means opening yourself up to others. But what about those *others,* the receivers? They really have to be there, or our generosity would have nowhere to go. Giving is only half the action, and if someone refuses what we offer, it hurts. Perhaps, then, some of us need to work at being generous receivers.

I have learned a lot about receiving from the women in the congregations we have served, for they have been such beautiful givers in my times of need. I have learned still more from a good friend, a woman my mother's age. For some wonderful, unknown reason, God must have put me "in her basket," because she has done so many generous, kind, and truly helpful things for me that I've lost count. And that's the way she wants it.

At first it was hard for me to accept so much generosity. My independent streak got in the way and I began to feel uncomfortably indebted to my friend. I wanted to return her love in tangible ways, and of course I couldn't. Being a sensitive person, she realized how I felt and one day she had a talk with me.

"Colleen, I get a lot of pleasure out of doing things for you," she said. "If only I didn't have to worry about your feeling of indebtedness. . . . Think of the fun I could have!" I couldn't believe it. She made me feel that I'd be doing her a favor by accepting her deeds of love.

I did a little thinking and a little praying, and gradually my attitude began to change. I put myself in my friend's place and realized how I would have felt if someone accepted my generosity with a frown on her face. And if a friend returned my favor tit for tat—like some kind of duty—it would make my generosity look like a pompous gesture done just for show. No—since my friend gave freely and lavishly of herself, responding to my needs as she saw them, the best way for me to be generous was to become a good receiver. For there is another part to the Beatitude, isn't there? *Happy are those who are generous. . . . God will be generous to them.*

There is so much God wants to give us. He wants to show

us how to make contact with people, how to express our love for our family, our friends, our fellow man, and for the whole world. And as we open up to each other, we will be more open to Him. Then His Spirit can move among us, soothing our cares, ministering to our hurts, uniting us in love, increasing our awareness of each other. In short, God wants to teach us how to be happy. That's too good an offer to turn down.

*Happy is the woman who is generous with her love and understanding. She knows that it isn't so much what she does, but what she is, that is really important to her loved ones. And when the voice of need is uttered, however feeble it may be, she hears it. She listens, she comforts, she supports, she gives her love generously. Because she becomes a part of the lives of those she loves, and because her happiness comes from her generosity, she receives even more than she gives.*

# 6

Happy are the utterly sincere, for they will see God!

Matthew 5:8 PHILLIPS

Blessed are the pure in heart: for they shall see God.

Matthew 5:8 KJV

# The Sincere Women

*Pure in heart ... pure in heart.* . . . What do these lovely, familiar words mean to me, a busy wife, a mother, a woman concerned about the world? Do they mean I am to be spotless, perfect? If so, I'll stop now—no need to go on.

But wait. Surely our Lord was describing something more —something more attainable for me. The concept of purity tumbles around in my mind. Then I look into the New Testament where I find that *purity* is mentioned twenty-seven times. Gradually I reject the idea that purity means perfection. Instead, it seems to mean genuineness, sincerity, honesty, a singleness of mind and purpose. Or, in the more concise words of Sören Kierkegaard, "Purity of heart is to will one thing."

*Transparent* is an even better word. Yes, I like that. To be pure in heart is to be a transparent person, a person with no shadows or double meanings, one who says what he means and means what he says. I like people who do that—people who don't hedge, who take a stand even if it turns out to be unpopular. I can think of many heroes who were transparent people.

But what about ordinary human beings meeting life's ordinary situations? What about someone like me?

I wasn't exactly transparent the other day, at least not at first. Going through the house, picking up the usual clutter, I came to one of our boys' rooms and stopped, surprised. The room was in perfect order! The bed was made, everything was put away, and each piece of furniture was where it belonged. I was so pleased.

When Tim came home from school I literally showered him with praise—"Good boy! You're a great guy to clean your room like that." He accepted my words casually. Well, I thought, we've always praised our children whenever we felt we could do it honestly, so why should he make a fuss over it?

I went back to my work, but something didn't feel right deep down inside me. *Pure in heart . . . pure in heart . . .* kept running through my mind. When you're pure in heart, you're honest about your feelings. You don't mean one thing and say another.

Well, I *was* honest, I told myself. I really do think Tim's a good guy. Yes, but "good" only because he cleaned his room? Did my son's goodness depend upon his neatness? No, of course not. That wasn't what I meant. Yet that's what I said.

It seemed like such a little thing, so I promised myself to remember it the next time I began to praise my son. Still, the not-right feeling persisted.

At that moment my son walked into the room.

"What I really meant was that you helped me a lot today by cleaning your room," I said. "My work was easier, and I felt you cared."

"Thanks." This time his response was warm and sincere, perhaps because I had become more real to him. My words of praise were related to a simple act, not to his entire being.

My son taught me something that day: I have to be transparent even in life's smallest moments. I have to express my true feelings, not the ones that rush in to cover up for what's really going on inside me.

That isn't easy to do today, when we live in a world that urges us to play it cool. "Don't wear your heart on your sleeve" —"Don't leave yourself wide open"—"Don't get involved." Sounds familiar, doesn't it? That's the kind of advice we all get from people who mean well. We may even catch ourselves saying the same words.

Jesus wasn't cool, and I don't think He wants us to be. When He calls us to become pure in heart, He's telling us that we have to take some risks. If we're going to express ourselves truly, honestly, that means we'll have to expose ourselves, be vulnerable. Someone may take advantage of us. We may be misunderstood. We may get hurt. That's part of being transparent. Nobody said it was easy.

I'm remembering one afternoon when I went shopping and got into a serious conversation with one of the store clerks. He was quite upset about the racial tensions in our nation, and particularly about the prospect of open housing. "They better not start coming in here," he said. "You wouldn't want one living next to you, would you?"

I liked that man and had known him for a long time. I didn't want to offend him, so it would have been easier for me to change the subject, pretending I didn't hear. But I did hear, and what he said troubled me. If I hadn't cared I could have passed off his comments. But I did care.

Gently, I tried to explain how I really felt—that "they" had every right to "come in here" or wherever they wanted to go—next door to me, or to him . . . that I hoped we all could begin to live as brothers and sisters, because we all are children of God.

The clerk was polite, but unmoved; our relationship became strained and it still is. Now I understand that reading sacred words is one thing, living them on a daily basis is something quite different. Expressing my real feelings may involve cost to me.

Perhaps, as I become more and more transparent, I will find ways to be open without offending. But perhaps not. Honesty is telling it like it is, and people don't always welcome it. At times I may have to hurt . . . or be hurt.

Jesus, I know You understand, because You lived through it. You weren't one of those "Now I have to be frank with you" persons who used truth like a dangerous weapon. But You *were* honest, no matter what it cost You. Remember when You told Peter that he would deny You? And he had just promised that he would never turn away from You. But You had to tell him the truth about himself, and later he understood why. You were telling Peter that he wasn't perfect, that he was even a coward at times—*and that You still loved him.*

Because You were honest, sometimes You had to hurt people . . . the scribes, the Pharisees, some of Your followers and Your dearest friends, even Your family. But Your honesty was always combined with love, and I think that's what made the difference. . . . You hurt only to heal, and everyone could see that love was Your motivation. It must also be mine.

Now I can see what You are telling me in this Beatitude. It's not enough for me to get rid of the shadows in myself. And it's not enough for people to be able to see clear through me.

They have to be able to see through me to something else. I must let God's love be visible through my transparency.

Wanting to express ourselves honestly doesn't make it happen. It's not that we're deceitful, at least not deliberately; but we're in the habit of speaking abstractly rather than personally. We've been taught that it's good manners to leave our feelings out of the things we say. And so we try to ignore our feelings entirely.

What a mistake that is! You can't ignore your emotions. Turn your back on them and they'll poke you in the ribs. Run away from them and they'll trip you. Slam a door in their faces and they'll break your windows.

Besides, what's so wrong about feelings, anyway? God gave us the capacity to feel and He must have had His reasons. Here in the Beatitudes He tells us how to appreciate feelings, understand them, and use them. He is reminding us that feelings can become vital lines of communication between one person and another. When we become transparent, there will be no obstacles between us.

Because it is so difficult for us to give up the defenses we put between ourselves and others, we need help in tearing them down. We just can't do it alone. That's why the pilgrimage toward transparency isn't a walk for loners. I know, because I've been on that journey for the past few years and I would have turned back many times had it not been for those who walked with me.

It's harder to lean than to be leaned on. It's harder to take the extended hand than to reach out with your own. It's easier to comfort than to allow ourselves to be comforted. We would rather dry someone else's tears than expose our own sorrows. And yet, we can't really reach someone else until we ourselves have been reached.

My family has helped me discover what my real feelings are. Now that the children are older, we have our own group encounters right around our dinner table—or anytime, for that matter. I remember one evening when I was in the kitchen packing the next day's lunches while my youngest son was keeping me company. I had the feeling that something was on his mind. He was talking casually about school, his friends, nothing in particular, until finally he got to the point. He was having a problem with one of his teachers. He couldn't put his finger on what it was, but he knew they were at cross-purposes and it bothered him.

I listened, wanting to help him sort out what he felt, but not knowing how. My impulse was to soothe him, to minimize the problem. . . . "Don't worry about it, son. It'll all work out"—"Maybe you're exaggerating the situation"—"Try not to think about it so much." No, that wasn't what I really felt, and I caught myself before I allowed the moment to slip by.

When Jamie began to talk about his problem, I remembered something that had happened to me a long time ago. For a split second I had an urge to share it with him, but I hesitated because it wasn't exactly my finest hour I was going to describe. Perhaps it's only human for us to want to present only the best parts of ourselves to our children, and so I almost hid my real self behind a lot of meaningless clichés. But then I realized that my son had had the courage to be honest with me. He had been totally transparent, and I simply had to respond to him in the same way.

So I told Jamie about a conflict I had had with one of my high-school teachers. It happened so long ago, yet as I described it I could still feel the pain of it.

I had a teacher who didn't like me. I'll never know why, because as far as I knew I had done nothing to earn her hostility. Perhaps I reminded her of someone else. Whatever the reason, she made my life miserable with her belittling remarks. I actually dreaded going to her class every day, knowing that she'd humiliate me in front of my friends.

It would have been wonderful to tell Jamie that I finally got

through to my teacher and that we had a nice, long talk that
cleared up all our misunderstandings. But that wasn't what
happened. No, I just had to suffer through that year in school
and go on to the next.

But I did learn something from that unhappy situation. Almost everyone I knew in school seemed to like me as much as
I liked them — but there were a few exceptions, and there always will be. Life is like that. Now and then you'll run into
someone who just doesn't like you, perhaps for reasons
neither of you can understand, and there isn't anything you
can do about it. Yes, it hurts, but that's all right. Life goes
on . . . and we can learn and grow through our hurts.

I could see that my son was interested and also a little surprised. He had heard (too often, I'm afraid) of my past suc-
cesses. But at that moment it was important for him to hear
about one of my failures because it made him realize that I
knew how he felt. There I was, standing at the sink while he
was sitting across the room, yet we were holding each other's
hand as surely as we ever had.

It's this self-censorship, this holding back of parts of ourselves that seems to be the greatest barrier between human
beings. I think it even prevents us from getting to know ourselves. Too often we build up false images of what we are
until we become convinced that they are real. Then it's especially hard to face the truth, to see ourselves clearly, transparently. We're afraid we won't like what we see, and we think
others will feel the same way. So we go along, handing out our
counterfeit selves — and then we wonder why we can't touch
each other anymore.

A few years ago several of our church members felt that
they wanted to reach out toward each other, but couldn't.
They decided that they needed help. And so they began —
very cautiously — to work with each other in small groups.

Now I know what the word *group* brings to mind. We think

of people behaving peculiarly, even sensationally, perhaps
letting too many restraints down along with their hair. We
thought of those things, too. But we went a little further and
found out that there are many kinds of groups, some more
constructive than others. It depends on what people want to
get out of them, who leads them, and what the members put
into them.

Our church groups have a distinct advantage. We don't
get together to tell each other sad stories; we aren't interested
in weird experiments; we aren't looking for company in our
misery. We are Christians trying to experience Jesus Christ
and His fellowship with one another. . . . We want to experience it more deeply and directly. We are seeking Him in
ourselves and in each other. In short, we are trying to help
each other become our genuine selves.

We're also lucky in that we have Gordon Hess, a young and
dedicated pastor with a real gift for group leadership. Gordy
has had a lot of experience in group encounter work, but he's
not what you'd call a "professional facilitator." Neither are the
rest of us professionals, and that's good, because we know we
are all in this life together . . . and there's no such thing as a
"professional person." As Gordy puts it, "Christ calls us to be
real, not religious. Our purpose is to hold hands with each
other as we walk through this difficult and sometimes lonely
life. Because we belong to God, we belong to each other — we
need each other."

In the beginning I had conflicting feelings about being in a
group. On the one hand I longed for the close-up fellowship
a small group offers, because in a large church there is such
a need for more than the Sunday-morning hello. But on the
other hand I was timid about this new experience. The truth
is, I was scared! But Gordy, sensitive friend that he is, forced
my hand by asking me to join the first training class for
leaders of small groups. Actually, that was our first group . . .

and once I got my feet wet, I was there to stay. Since then I've
been involved in women's daytime groups. Women from nine-
teen to seventy have been transformed from faces in the
Sunday-morning crowd to my sisters in Christ, with whom
I share life. The love that flows among us is a very special
gift from God.

The groups I have been in over the past few years have
been honest and supportive. There have been painful moments when I was forced to look at the flaws in my being
which the others helped me to see . . . but even then I knew
that I was loved and accepted as a person created by God.
And there have been moments of utter joy over the discovery
of something worthwhile that I could share with others.

It has taken time and patience, but in our group work we
have learned to express our fears, our hang-ups, our delights.
Gradually we are able to express the most important part of
ourselves—our love for God and for one another. At last we
are coming to the place where we can share each other's
burdens (Galatians 6), which is what Christians are meant to
do. Prayer has also been a very real part of our experience,
and believe me, after the searching moments we share with
each other, our prayers are not just a lot of pretty words.
They are real, and they come from deep within us.

Some amazing things have happened to us as we became
more honest with each other. I have seen personalities
emerge and spiritual wounds heal as we allowed Christ and
His kind of honesty to work through us.

Anne's experience is a good example of what can happen
in a Christian group. The first time I spoke to her we were
total strangers. She and her husband had serious problems
and, having heard about our church groups, she called me to
ask about them. She sounded desperate, and when she began
to cry I nearly lost my own composure. We couldn't accomplish much on the telephone, so we arranged to meet a few
days later.

Anne and her husband Carl had been married about twenty years. They had four fine children and a home that appeared — from the outside, at least — to be happy and secure. Anne and Carl were very close and their love for each other was deep — no problem there. When it came to sharing their faith, that was something else.

It was startling for them to realize that they had such a problem at all, considering their backgrounds. Both came from Christian homes. When they met, Anne was the daughter of a minister and Carl was a young seminarian interning in her father's church. They fell in love and were married when Carl graduated from seminary. Anne, at eighteen, went from minister's daughter to minister's wife, a simple enough transition — or so she thought.

She kept telling herself that her life was trouble-free. And why shouldn't it be? She knew all the answers — she had memorized enough Bible verses to fit anything life might bring her way, she could study the Scriptures in depth and find their prescriptions for her problems, and she knew every hymn in the book. Going through the motions of her role was a snap.

But inside Anne there was another person — a woman who could not squeeze life into a narrow mold. This inner person needed more than memorized Bible passages to sustain her faith. She needed to know the living Christ Himself and to feel His influence in her life. And, not understanding how to reach out to Him, she waited for His touch. When it didn't come, she began to doubt that He existed.

The doubts increased secretly for many years until finally Anne couldn't stand being a skin-deep Christian any longer. One day she told her husband how she felt. Understandably, Carl was hurt and confused. Never having known such doubts himself he was unable to deal with Anne's. He seemed to think he could compensate for her loss of faith by spending more and more hours alone in his study praying, reading the

Bible, and meditating. Rejected and filled with guilt, Anne rebelled against religion altogether—no worship, no prayer, no mention of God.

Everything else in her life began to come apart after that. She and Carl disagreed on how to bring up their children. Carl, a gentle, loving parent, seemed to get closer to the children, whereas Anne, a strict disciplinarian, felt she was turning them off.

The reason Anne decided to get in touch with one of our church groups was that she had a particularly serious argument with her husband. As usual it led to a discussion of Anne's doubts about God. As she was trying to explain them, Carl interrupted her angrily. "For God's sake and the children's, find out what you *do* believe!" he said. He asked her if she realized what a bad example she was setting for their children. Filled with hatred for herself and convinced that she was a failure as a mother, Anne ran to her bedroom. Sobbing, not even realizing what she was doing, she began to cry out to God, asking Him to show her where to turn. That's when she remembered reading about the work our groups were doing.

Anne was such an unhappy woman when I met her. Just talking about her problems was a big step for her to take, and I admired her courage. It meant that she had to come out from behind the facade that had sheltered and imprisoned her all her life. She was presenting herself—doubts and all—as honestly as she possibly could. It was not an easy thing to do, especially by herself. What made it even more difficult was that Anne saw herself as an ugly, unlovable person—when, in fact, she was truly lovely.

I reached out and touched her. "You're coming into your own as an individual, Anne. That's wonderful!"

She was quite surprised. I could see that she expected some sort of reprimand.

"It's all right," I said. "God meant you to be an individual — it's about time you got to know yourself the way He does."

Still she couldn't believe her ears. I understood how she felt. I had seen this happen many times in our group — it had happened to me.

"God loves you very much, Anne," I told her. "And He loves you the way you are. So do I."

She began to cry again, but this time they were tears of relief. I suggested that she join one of our women's groups where she would have the help and support she needed as she searched for her authentic self. I could see that the prospect was both promising and frightening. It was like a door held open to her, a door that led to — who knows? For a moment she struggled with her fears and then she won out over them.

That night Anne told her husband about joining the group. When she saw the tears come to his eyes she realized how much she had been hurting him over the years — and how much he really loved her! Holding each other tightly, they felt the warmth and deep sense of caring that had been missing for a long time. Changes were already happening in Anne's life.

Our women's group helped Anne in many ways. "They accepted me even when I told them about my doubts of God," she said. But she still found it hard to share her problems with Carl. His self-confidence and his complete spiritual tranquillity made her ashamed of her own uneasiness. Gradually Anne began to realize that the best way to communicate with her husband was for both of them to join a couples' group where they could face their problems together.

It worked. As the communication lines between husband and wife began to open, they revealed that Anne wasn't the only one with problems. Carl had a few of his own, and as he became more aware of them he began to sympathize with what Anne had been experiencing. She was no longer alone.

During the past year Anne and Carl have faced situations and crises that would have wrecked them if they had remained so far apart. But now they are able to help each other through life's rougher moments. They not only feel their love for each other — they *live* it.

Their children have gained most of all. Anne and Carl can see now that the most important thing they can do is to let their children know how much they love them. If they have different ways of showing their love, it doesn't seem to matter — the children know how they feel.

And God? Somehow, through receiving God's love as it came to her through others, Anne has found God. She has had the encounter she desperately needed and it has given her the courage to be herself. She is not afraid to let others see the person God created. In other words, she is becoming a transparent human being.

"Sharing my faith and my life with friends who really care has been the most wonderful experience of my life," she told me recently. "I feel as if I'm floating on a cloud of friendship — a deep, warm friendship with Jesus."

Now you can understand why I'm convinced that Christ-centered groups can be a real help along our pilgrimage to transparency. Anne is one example, and there have been many others. Of course, group work is only one way, and it's not for everyone. A good friend of ours, who has come alive as a person and a believer during the past few years, says, "I don't need a group — my whole life has become a group experience." And he's right — just being with him is an exciting encounter with honesty. This should be the end result of every group experience as well.

It really doesn't matter how you become a transparent person. The important thing is that it happens. And when it does it will turn your life into a daily adventure as all the routine, familiar things take on new and deeper meaning.

The other day I saw what a difference it made when I applied Jesus' concept of honesty to a very small incident. It was panic hour at our house, which means that I was preparing dinner, the children and their friends were home from school, and the telephone was ringing endlessly. One call was from a new young woman in our church who asked me to attend a women's meeting with her later that week.

It sounded like fun, except that I already had a full week. So I hedged, but I felt pressure in return. I knew that if I said *yes* my family would get the short end of the bargain. This was not my season to major in ladies' meetings, yet I felt the old temptation to give in to social pressures in order to please my caller. And then I reminded myself — *to be pure in heart is to be perfectly honest about your feelings.* I decided to say *no* and explain why.

At first there was nothing but silence at the other end of the line. Then the young woman said, "Well, it's a good thing you're a minister's wife today and not fifty years ago when ministers' wives were not only asked but *expected* to do everything!"

My own honesty was such a relief that I was able to appreciate hers. "It sure is," I said, and laughed.

She laughed too. We talked on — she understood. She might not have but she did. And I had a new friend.

At dinner that night I felt unusually gay and free. Conversation was animated and the children were hilarious. We all felt especially close to each other. Our happy time lingered on into the after-dinner hours of cleanup, homework, lunch packing — often the hours that take the last bit of starch out of a wilted day.

Later, when the house was quiet, the children asleep, and my husband still busy at the church, I saw that my Bible was open to Matthew 5 where I had been reading earlier in the day — *Happy are the pure in heart . . . the transparent people.* Truly, God had spoken to me through His Word.

As I looked ahead to the next day I found myself wonder-

ing what new adventures were in store for me. And so it can
be — for all of us, each day of our lives.

*Happy is the woman who is honest with herself, with others, and,
above all, with God. This woman has given over every conscious
area of her life to God, and has asked Him to reveal to her the inner
areas of fear and bitterness that need to be healed. Between her and
her fellow human beings, there is no barrier. In her there is no ten-
sion, for she seeks to hide nothing from God or man. Because she is a
transparent person, her Lord is able to shine through her life and be
visible to those around her.*

(Portions of Chapter 6 are paraphrased material reprinted by permission
from *Guideposts* magazine. Copyright © 1968 by Guideposts Associates, Inc.,
Carmel, New York 10512.)

# 7

Happy are those who make peace, for they will
be known as sons of God!

Matthew 5:9 PHILLIPS

Blessed are the peacemakers: for they shall be
called the children of God.

Matthew 5:9 KJV

# The Peacemaking Women

PEACE . . . ah, yes, we see the word often these days—in
symbols, on bumper stickers, on Christmas cards, and on
buildings. One friend of ours uses it on his personal statio-
nery, another has it written boldly across his front door. It's
all around us—yet, what is it, this *peace?* And who are today's
peacemakers? Whoever they are, Jesus says they are happy
people, and they belong to Him. *Happy are the peacemakers . . .
they are the children of God.*

Is peace something quiet, unruffled—perhaps unreachable? Are the peacemakers those calm, unshakable people
I often wish I could be like? And is there really a place for
peace in this turbulent, pulsating world?

The word *peace* makes me think of summer vacations, of

long hours when at last I don't have anything special to do;
when the weather is warm and beautiful and I have the time
to hear the breeze moving in the trees. Yes, that's peaceful —
but throw in a little rainstorm . . . let school begin again and
fill my days with busy moments, and exit peace! At least, *that*
kind of peace.

But that's okay — because that's not the kind of peace Jesus
is talking about in this Beatitude. The peace we find in this
world is totally dependent upon time, place, and circum-
stance. It comes and it goes. Jesus was talking about *real* peace,
the peace that comes from God. He spelled it out for us: "I
leave behind with you — peace; I give you my own peace and
my gift is nothing like the peace of this world" (John 14:27).
Once we have God's peace, it doesn't leave us, no matter what
happens in our lives or in the world around us. It's always
there, deep inside us. God's peace is . . . a sense of occupancy
in the heart . . . a feeling that Someone is there all the time —
a spiritual reaching out for God's hand and finding it there.
That is peace.

Surely, then, if we are to become peacemakers, we must
first of all be at peace with ourselves. For if we're at war on the
inside, we'll carry the battle out into the world. As Jesus said,
"If a household is divided against itself, it cannot last"
(Mark 3:25). And neither can we — our inner conflicts can
bring the walls of our being down around our ears.

That's what happened to some people I knew years ago.
They were very unhappy in their church because they ob-
jected to the minister's "politics in the pulpit." For instance,
one Sunday he asked them if they could buy love and justice —
and they thought the love theme sounded a bit like some kind
of Communist propaganda. They thought a preacher should
preach the gospel — but apparently without applying it to life.

Well, they left the church and went to another one that was
known for its strict emphasis on worship and its lack of social

involvement. But still they weren't happy. They had just as many complaints, although for different reasons. It was obvious that these people would never find peace anywhere until they found it within themselves. Wherever they went, they took their inner frustrations with them . . . and they became disturbers of peace.

When Jesus lives within us, His love brings the warring elements of our selves together into the whole persons we were meant to be. He frees us to be the "you" of you and the "me" of me. We can shake hands with our selves . . . we have peace.

There's also something about inner peace that makes us want to spread it around. We want to bring it into our relationships with other people and eliminate the barriers between us. But that isn't always easy, and sometimes the process isn't what we usually think of as "peaceful." It may mean uncomfortable, even painful exchanges between us.

A few years ago Louie and I were visiting friends from another parish we had served. It was what we call a "warm-fuzzy" night—comfortable old friends combined with interesting new people to meet.

At Louie's table there were several new acquaintances . . . one of them was a gifted artist whose work we both admired (but couldn't afford). Her name was Gail and she was a lovely woman, full of grace as a person. From her husband, with whom I was sitting, I learned that she also had a busy home life—when I asked about the size of their family, his answer was simply, "Boys—and numerous!"

Gail seemed to be a gal with everything. But of course we didn't know what was going on inside her . . . and at that moment she was in the midst of a terrible struggle between her home and her career. At first she had thought she could handle them both—and do a creditable job in each area. Then came the days when she couldn't cope, and the short straw always seemed to go to the boys and her husband.

Actually we all have days like that, even when we don't have a budding career to squeeze into our lives. But Gail was convinced that she was having more than a healthy share of difficulty and she was afraid it was hurting her family. And so, the night we met her she was carrying a heavy burden of guilt in her heart.

I didn't know how Gail felt until about a year later. Louie was one of the speakers at a regional ecumenical retreat, and Gail and her husband were there representing their church. It was wonderful to see them again, and I was especially delighted to learn that Gail and I were in the same small group which was to meet every morning for discussion and sharing.

At our group's first morning meeting we went from one to another, trying to put words around who we felt we were and what we thought was our main priority as a Christ person. Everyone shared—except Gail. Throughout the meeting she blinked back tears. No one questioned her, but her silence let us know she was hurting. After the meeting she stayed behind, and I could see that she wanted to talk. When we were alone she told me what was bothering her. . . . And would you believe it? *It was my husband!*

Apparently, at that "warm-fuzzy" dinner party almost a year ago, Louie had said something that had cut Gail deeply . . . had seemed almost cruel. He had spoken of the need to balance career and family . . . and of the danger that a profession might take up all of a person's life energy, leaving human relationships, and the family in particular, with the crumbs from the table. His remarks seemed innocuous enough, but to Gail—at that sensitive moment in her life— they were crushing. Her mind began to play tricks with her. . . . "Louie knew something"—he didn't. "My husband must have talked to him"—he hadn't. "Louie thinks women shouldn't have careers"—wrong again! Silently, all those months, Gail had kept her hurt inside herself until now it had festered and grown out of proportion.

I understood what Gail had done, for I could remember doing the same thing . . . being hurt, usually through a misunderstanding, and instead of talking it out immediately, I embraced the hurt feelings—suffering inside for days, weeks, even months. Why do we do such things, when it's so much nicer to embrace a friend instead of a hurt?

Clearly, Gail had misunderstood Louie. I knew his feelings on the subject, and I realized that he hadn't been talking to Gail specifically, nor to women in general. He was speaking about all people . . . about businessmen who make money their god, about ministers who make success their thing—about himself and me, for we were having our own struggle to keep the balance between work and family.

During those months Gail had felt guilty and censured—and so unnecessarily. I tried to tell her that, but she wasn't about to be convinced, at least not by me.

It was a long day, waiting to see Louie alone. First there was lunch, and then the "discipline of silence" until dinner. (That really *was* a discipline for me that day!) Next came dinner, then evening vespers—and finally, cabin time! At last I could tell Louie about Gail.

When I told him, he was concerned . . . concerned that Gail had been hurting for so long . . . concerned that she was hurting still. Late as it was, he grabbed his flashlight and went looking for the cabin where Gail and her husband were staying. He was gone a long time and I fell sound asleep.

The next morning at breakfast Gail's husband—a gentle giant of a man—rushed up to us and hugged Louie. "Louie, Louie," he said, "there is peace between my house and yours!"

Peace had been made the night before when Gail and Louie talked out their misunderstanding on the porch of Gail's cabin. At first it had been awkward and difficult for both of them. Now they were very tired and would need an extra cup of coffee. But the important thing was that they had been willing to suffer the discomfort that led to mutual under-standing . . . to *shalom,* the peace that comes after the honest struggle. And then, as they talked, they really heard each other . . . they had become peacemakers.

Only when we have peace within ourselves can we mend these breaks in our relationships with others. Only when Jesus makes us whole can we begin to see that the world itself needs to be made whole.

A peacemaker is an absorbent person. When malicious words and gossip hit him, they go no further. . . . Instead of reverberating in excitement, he is like a great silencing cham-ber . . . gossip hits him and is absorbed. Yes, he may feel the sting of it, but he doesn't pass it on. He smothers it with for-giveness.

I'll never forget seeing such a magnanimous spirit in action. Some years ago, while Louie and I were studying in Scotland, Billy Graham came to London to hold a crusade at the Har-ringay Arena. Since we had known Billy and the team back home, we were asked to come from Edinburgh to work with Dawson Trotman in follow-up—which we did for eight won-derful weeks.

One night several of us squeezed into a small British car to accompany Billy to the arena. Billy was preaching that night and I remember wishing he could have had a quieter ride, but we were excited and talkative. Then one of our group began to tell Billy about some unkind, terribly unfair comments an ecclesiastical leader had made about him in the newspapers. Apparently our fellow passenger felt it his duty to repeat them to Billy, but believe me, if I'd had a muzzle I'd have used it! I felt hurt for Billy and I wondered how he could possibly get up and preach after hearing such things.

For a long time Billy sat quietly. Then, thoughtfully and simply, as though he were speaking partly to us and partly to Someone Else, he said, "God bless that man. If I were in his place, I'd probably feel the same way about me."

As far as Louie and I can recall, that was all he said — but we have never forgotten it. Many times, finding ourselves in similar situations, it has helped us to remember his words and his attitude. (Thank you, Billy!)

Jesus, now I understand what You meant when You said, "Love your enemies, bless them that curse you . . ." (Matthew 5:44 KJV). I always wondered how I could throw my arms around someone who deliberately hurt me. But now I know that it *is* possible — if I am a peacemaker. There is a difference between the action and the person . . . I don't have to love them both. You are telling me to love *the person.*

Peace in our mind . . . peace in our close relationships . . . that's a good beginning. But if peace ends there — on the inside — something is *very* wrong. Peace is a precious commodity, a part of our inheritance in Christ, but if we seek it simply for our own comfort, it will lose its purpose.

We must remember that we aren't called to *keep* peace, but to *make* peace. The inner peace Jesus gives us equips us to go out into the world and bring its warring forces together.

Keeping peace is passive . . . "Don't rock the boat" — "Don't get involved in controversy" — "Sweep unpleasantness under the rug." Peace keepers often hide from problems, crying "Peace, peace!" when there is no peace, and no one to make it. By ignoring conflicts, they actually make them worse.

"Making peace" is active, involved, aggressive. Peacemakers can see past personalities to the issues that must be resolved. They are strong people who can take moral stands. They bring sanity out of chaos and confusion.

Sometimes it takes more than one person to make things

whole. In our town the University on occasion will hold open meetings where people with conflicting views can discuss a controversial issue. Our congregation also holds open forums that serve a similar purpose . . . they give people an opportunity to speak out on some highly emotional subjects.

But sometimes our discussions get pretty heated, and at times it seems that we're only making a situation worse by talking about it. Then—always from somewhere among us—comes a peacemaker, a person whose vision extends far beyond our personal interests to where the real problem lies. His clarity of mind, his integrity, and his courage seem to lift the rest of us up to his level where we, too, can see more clearly.

Yes, our world needs peacemakers. Not only do they bring us together—they also seem to bring out the good in us all. And perhaps that's the element that will hold the pieces of this world together someday. . . .

As I go through the house straightening up, I like to let my mind run free. One morning recently I was thinking about peacemakers. . . . Who are they? I mean, specifically—what do they do in life? What do they look like? Where would we find one if we needed one? And how would we recognize one in a crowd?

Certainly a sincere evangelist is a peacemaker. His entire life is given over to reconciling man to God through Christ. But we all can't be evangelists in that sense, can we? Some of us—many of us—have no talent for speaking to masses of people . . . some of us must simply let God's peace work in our lives and pray that it will fall like good seed in the lives of those we touch each day. If we use every opportunity we have to bring man closer to God and man closer to man, then *we* are the peacemakers—each one of us.

My thoughts were interrupted when the phone rang. It

was Sue, a friend I don't see very often . . . actually, I don't have to, because our friendship is always there when either of us needs it. That day Sue needed it . . . she was crying. I waited, not knowing what to say, but I used those moments to pray for my friend and for Ed, her husband. Their marriage had been in trouble for years. They had serious financial problems and both of them were working to keep their two older children in college. . . . There was a crisis in the life of a younger child . . . and during the past few years there had been a siege of illness and surgery in the family. Life had been rough for Sue and Ed, and instead of bringing husband and wife closer together—as rough times can do—it had driven them far apart.

When Sue got control of her tears and was able to talk, she told me that their situation had come to a head the previous day. She and Ed had a terrible argument. In desperation they went to a mutual friend of theirs and ours—a minister who is now a clinical psychologist. This man is truly gifted by God in the art of counseling, and generously filled with the love of the Holy Spirit. He was just what Sue and Ed needed.

First, he asked Sue and Ed to be specific about all the things they resented in each other. Painful and humiliating as it must have been, they did it . . . and there it was—all the years of ugliness and hurt out in the open.

Then the counselor asked them to be equally specific in describing all the good things they saw in each other . . . the things that had drawn them together in the beginning, the things that had made their marriage last for twenty years, and the things that were still there. And as they probed among the ruins of their life, they began to see that there was still a lot to love in each other. As Sue put it, "We really have so much to go on."

I realized then that Sue's tears came from joy, from the relief of knowing that she and Ed could become whole again, in time. Our friend the psychologist had been the peacemaker in their fragmented relationship.

Now Sue and I prayed for God's final touch of healing, for she and Ed had done many things to hurt each other, in the way that only a husband and wife can hurt, and there was a deep need for forgiveness on each side. But they would have help. Jesus is the expert Forgiver and Forgetter, and because He had come to live *in* them, He would do this *for* them.

I hung up the phone with a feeling of gratitude for all peacemakers everywhere. And I prayed that when I had the opportunity to serve, I would be ready.


Ready? Am I ready now? There really isn't any perfect time to be ready to bring people together. Jesus is always ready . . . we simply have to let Him use us.

But some conflicts are so big . . . where do we begin to reconcile them? I'm thinking about war . . . after all, you can't really think about peace without thinking about war. What can I do about it? What can we ordinary people do to end war?

I hate war . . . so does everyone I know. The fact that I have three sons may have something to do with the intensity of my feelings. Yet I felt the same way before I had sons. But I also hate tyranny and manipulation of persons . . . there lies the moral conflict each of us must work out for himself.

Still, there are things we can do as peacemakers. We can pray for the leaders of our nation and for those of all other nations. We can pray for the men and women who have the enormous responsibility of making decisions that affect the lives of so many others. May they be sensitive to the forces that lead to peace . . . may they be strong enough to suffer the discomfort of reconciling differences . . . may they *respect*

honest differences and not make conformity their only aim
. . . may they, too, pray for guidance.

War does more than kill. It commits atrocities on the hearts
and minds of the people who stay behind while their sons go
off to fight. A Japanese-American friend of ours went
through a cruel ordeal during World War II. One day he was
a respected friend and neighbor—and the next day he was
whisked off to an internment camp as a so-called national
security risk. Many German-Americans suffered similar experiences. After the war, the Russians became the bad guys
. . . and then the Chinese. That's what happens when we
allow ourselves to become part of war's hate syndrome.

We can support our country without hating those who dis-
agree with its policies . . . because, for peacemakers, there is
no enemy. We can aim to be like Jesus, hating the forces that
cause war, but never hating our fellow human beings who are
caught up in it.

But wars don't have to start . . . we don't have to hate or
destroy. There is another Way. . . .

In the closing scene of the film version of the novel *Ben Hur*,
the young Palestinian Judah Ben Hur is reached by Jesus the
Christ. And Judah, a man whose life had been filled with hate,
bitterness, and revenge, says simply, "He has taken the sword
out of my hand." That's exactly what Jesus does when He
comes into our lives. He takes the swords out of our hands.
We no longer want to hurt . . . we want to heal. With His
love in our hearts, we shall be able to make peace . . . and as
God's children, we shall be unable to make war. That's the
other Way. . . . At least, in my own personal struggle of con-
science, so it is for me.

*Happy is the woman who truly longs for peace—within herself,
within her family, and throughout the world. For she knows that
strife begins within the human soul where parts of ourselves are at*

*war against each other. Beginning with herself, she asks God to help her end the conflicts that lead to destruction. From there, she seeks to reconcile the differences that exist among all human beings, even in the midst of love . . . perhaps even in her own family. Deeply happy is this woman when she sees that God is the Way to peace, and that through her words and witness she can be used by Him as a peacemaker.*

# 8

Happy are those who have suffered persecution
for the cause of goodness, for the kingdom of
heaven is theirs!
And what happiness will be yours when people
blame you and ill-treat you and say all kinds of
slanderous things against you for my sake! Be
glad then, yes, be tremendously glad — for your
reward in heaven is magnificent. They persecuted the prophets before your time in exactly
the same way.

Matthew 5:10–12 PHILLIPS

Blessed are they which are persecuted for righteousness' sake: for theirs is the kingdom of
heaven.
Blessed are ye, when men shall revile you, and
persecute you, and shall say all manner of evil
against you falsely, for my sake.
Rejoice, and be exceeding glad: for great is
your reward in heaven: for so persecuted they
the prophets which were before you.

Matthew 5:10–12 KJV

# The Suffering Women

*Persecution* . . . what a grim word. I don't even want to think
about it. I flinch from it . . . it reminds me of the early Christians and the suffering they endured.

But persecution still exists, and many of us later Christians
suffer for our faith. The acts of torment are more subtle
than those the Romans used, but they can be very painful

. . . the social stigma we're given when we refuse to join organizations that exclude certain people . . . the looks of guests at a dinner party when we don't laugh at their dehumanizing jokes . . . the ridicule a young person gets when he refuses to go along with the group in unhealthy experiments. Love itself disturbs some people.

Chip, chip, chip — that's the way it goes these days . . . hundreds of little persecutions that chip away at our spiritual complacency, reminding us that we are not our own. We belong to Jesus, and there is a price we must pay. . . .

If we're humble — the proud and arrogant will call us foolish.

If we're tamed by God — those who are self-made will call us weak.

If we're transparently honest — we will irritate those who feel uncomfortable with the truth.

If we're generous, and those around us seek revenge — we'll be known as a soft touch.

If we believe that God's ways are the best ways for mankind — we'll be called prudes.

If we're peacemakers when others want war — we'll be called weaklings, even traitors.

Just as Jesus was persecuted, His followers will meet with opposition along the Way. Unavoidably the Christian life will be a rebuke to some — and people don't take kindly to being rebuked.

Christians were made to give and receive love — not to hate or lie in wait for an enemy. That's why, of all things in life, persecution is the hardest for us to bear.

But why does anyone have to suffer? Is it God's way of reprimanding us when we do something wrong? And if we do all the right things, will we automatically be exempt from this pain?

Intellectually we all know that the answer to those questions is *no*. Yet we often behave as if it were *yes*. Let suffering come into our lives and we begin saying, "What have I done wrong?" Or worse than that—"Why is God punishing me?"

Suffering is a stubborn fact of human life. It comes to everyone, without discrimination. But not all suffering has value—what we suffer *for* can make a difference. Jesus didn't say, *Happy are you when you suffer*—period. He said, *Happy are you when you suffer for right causes.*

If I were to tally the score, I'm sure I'd find that most of my suffering has come from doing something wrong to my brothers and sisters in life and not from doing something right for God. I have goofed more often than I like to admit . . . I've been thoughtless . . . I've hurt people . . . I've been selfish . . . and when I realize what I've done, I suffer. There is no joy in this kind of pain.

But even when I make careless mistakes I can feel God at work in me . . . showing me my weaknesses . . . pushing me to admit I was wrong . . . stretching me . . . and then finally giving me the grace to forgive myself. So there is some good in this kind of suffering, after all—yet it's not the kind Jesus is describing in this final Beatitude. When He says we will find joy through our pain, He is speaking about the kind of suffering we will know only when we stand with Him and walk His Way. It is the outcome of *living* the Beatitudes.

How easy it is for me to nod my head and say, "Yes, that's right!" Making it part of my life is something else. I find it very hard. When Jesus tells me not only to anticipate trouble but to "jump for joy" when it comes—that's hard. It will mean far more than nodding my head.

I think of Joachim, a man we met in a work camp in Europe some years ago. . . . He and his family suffered the loss of many material things because he was determined to fulfill his call to preach the gospel.

I think of our friends who, because they are Christians, are speaking out against white supremacy in countries where it is a government policy. They are suffering as a result. In a recent letter one of them assured us, "Please believe that we are all in good heart. Our Christian faith, thank God, enables us to face persecution with equanimity and cheerfulness."

I think of the martyred Stephen in the Book of Acts. . . . I think of the African evangelist who spoke to our congregation recently and told us about the persecution Christians have suffered in many parts of his continent . . . and how they were filled with forgiving love for their persecutors even in the midst of their agony.

Yes, even today some Christians are giving their lives for Jesus Christ . . . and good things *do* come out of suffering when He is present.

I think of Corrie ten Boom and her sister, Betsie, imprisoned in the terrible concentration camp, Ravensbruck, during World War II . . . two brave Dutch women enduring inhuman brutality and coming through it spiritually triumphant. In *The Hiding Place* Corrie ten Boom describes her prison ordeal and the amazing change that came into her life:

> But as the rest of the world grew stranger, one thing became increasingly clear. And that was the reason the two of us were here. Why others should suffer we were not shown. As for us, from morning until lights-out, whenever we were not in ranks for roll call, our Bible was the center of an ever-widening circle of help and hope. Like waifs clustered around a blazing fire, we gathered about it, holding out our hearts to its warmth and light. The blacker the night around us grew, the brighter and truer and more beautiful burned the word of God. "Who shall separate us from the love of Christ? Shall tribulation, or distress, or persecution, or famine, or nakedness, or peril, or sword? . . . Nay, in all these things we are more than conquerors through Him that loved us."
>
> I would look about us as Betsie read, watching the light leap

from face to face. More than conquerors. . . . It was not a wish. It was a fact. We knew it, we experienced it minute by minute—poor, hated, hungry. We are more than conquerors. Not "we shall be." We are! Life in Ravensbruck took place on two separate levels, mutually impossible. One, the observable, external life, grew every day more horrible. The other, the life we lived with God, grew daily better, truth upon truth, glory upon glory.

God invaded Corrie ten Boom's time of persecution, and He will do the same for us—*whenever our cause is right.* Few of us will ever go to prison for our faith, but at some point in our lives persecution will present us with a choice—do we enter in or back away? do we say *yes* or *no?* do we live or die? And by that, I don't mean only physical death, for there are other ways to die.

If we believe that the cause is right, if we are willing to suffer for the moment because God has given us eyes to see beyond now to what will follow, what then? What help will there be? What guarantee do we have that we will find strength, peace, and joy at the end of the road?

A very good friend who has known more than a little suffering in life says, "We all will suffer persecution if we follow Jesus—but we must choose our hill wisely." In other words, we must be sure in our hearts that the cause we are willing to suffer for is His. For without His presence, there can be no joy in suffering.

But if we believe that the cause is God's—what then? How can we be sure He'll stand with us?

At this point I feel a little inadequate to write about this Beatitude. So many others could speak with depth of their experiences, while mine seem shallow. But Jesus doesn't tell us to *seek* suffering and persecution—only to expect it, accept it, and find joy in it when it comes. The portion that has come to me is small, and couldn't really be called persecution, but in my times of suffering God *has* brought me a strange kind of joy, and this is what I want to share. . . .

One day, without warning, it happens—you're not looking for trouble . . . you don't want to make waves . . . but all of a sudden you have to put your faith where your mouth is. . . . You do something that seems simple, uncompromising— and the world turns upside down. . . .

A few years ago we moved to a new church in a very beautiful, very affluent town. The town was changing . . . research centers were popping up all over the area, and the University of California had built a campus there. New industry brought new people, new ideas, new life-styles. Clearly, the town was on the growing edge of a changing American society. Its newness was part of what drew us there . . . it was also what repelled many of the established residents. That's the *where* of the situation. Add to this the *when*—the year of a bitter debate concerning open housing in California which wasn't the most welcome subject in a town where there were reports of a so-called gentlemen's agreement to keep "certain elements" out. And the *who?* The new minister and his wife, who didn't have the sense to do as they were told and stay away from controversy.

Within a short time after our installation Louie preached a group of sermons that applied the gospel to life—to *our* life in *our* town! In one sermon he read from Colossians 3:11: *In Christ there is no Jew or Greek, male or female—we are all one.* And then he ended with a question. . . . If we believed in this oneness, could we actually deny *anything*—housing, jobs, education—to *anyone?*

A few weeks earlier I had been asked to join an Open Housing committee, and of course I did. I worked with some of our most dedicated citizens—dowagers, domestics, faculty wives, realtors, and just plain *hausfraus* like me. I had no idea

I was headed for trouble until one day there was a picture of our committee in the newspaper. Immediately a member of our congregation took me aside and said, "No minister's wife should ever get involved in such a controversial thing!"

Well, Louie did, and I did, and now the repercussions began. First there were phone calls from friends who felt sorry for us . . . then there were angry callers who wanted to put us in our place. On the Sunday Louie preached on Colossians 3:11 I just got back to the house when the phone rang—it was my first obscene call! I guess I'm pretty "cream cheese" because I was so shocked, all I could say was, "Why, sir! God bless you!" and hang up. Then there was the message telling us, "Go back to Harlem where you belong" . . . and the endless stream of hate literature, parts of it underlined especially for us.

It went on for months. Normally I'm a mail hound, but by that time I dreaded going to the mailbox. And there were other things, too—things that were hard to take, because they hit my vulnerability center—my family.

In the beginning, when Louie became aware of the hostility, he was angry. I remember walking the beach with him for hours . . . we were asking ourselves—and God—if this was one of those times when we were to shake the dust from our feet and move on. There were places to move on to, and certainly we were tempted, but always the sense of call and the urgency to do a job right where we were won out. Our decision was simply to do as the gospel says—and take the consequences.

Then I saw something happen in Louie's life. . . . Something was coming in from the outside. His times of quiet and prayer were rewarded with peace and love . . . peace regarding what had happened, love for the opposition. It didn't seem natural—that's what I mean by "Something from outside." It was Christ's own Spirit.

I knew then that the cause was right. There would be no turning back.

That was eight years ago, and I wish I could tell you that once we turned the corner, everything was beautiful. Everything wasn't, but many things began to be.

It was still hard to lose people because they didn't like a church that was "involved"—but it was good to gain new people who wanted a church precisely because it was. It was still hard to accept bigotry in some people—yet it was so good to find that in some people it wasn't bigotry at all, but rather an honest difference of opinion as to the role the church is to play in the world. It was still hard to be criticized by the fringes of the community, one side calling us "radical com-symps" and the other "gradualists"—but it was good to sense an inner freedom that caused us to care less about what either side said. It was more important that people had the time and the opportunity to change.

And through all these glad-sad years, many exciting things were happening—the Greater Parish Ministry, born of our Minister of Missions' dream of churches working together to meet the human needs of *our* people in *our* city . . . lay people trained and sent out as evangelists in our own congregation and community . . . new classes to make the mind stretch . . . a new contemporary worship service added to the two traditional Sunday-morning services . . . on Friday nights a chapel service of prayer and praise led by laymen . . . a youth program that makes your spirit zing, as young people from the church and from the streets of our town come together in the Sun House, getting to know each other and their Lord . . . the choirs growing in all ways, young people encouraged and trained to use their talents for God—their flutes, recorders, violins, bells, trumpets, and guitars—surprising us with joy in our services . . . and best of all—*love* . . . love being felt and expressed, love touching and healing lives . . . a true baptism of love through the Holy Spirit.

Yes, during all these years God has been at work, and probably more in us than anywhere else. We have been pulled and pushed and made to grow, and He has been more than faithful. He has never left us without help.

During our most difficult days, help came in many forms, most of them unexpected. God was telling us that we weren't alone.

One Sunday a visiting minister came to speak at our church. He was a man everyone loved and respected. Although I had never met him, it took all of two minutes after our introduction to make me feel he and I had been friends for a long time. He was old enough to be my father, widely traveled, and very charming.

Our guest was easy to talk to and as we lingered over Sunday dinner Louie and I told him about the crisis in our lives. If we were looking for sympathy—and I suppose we were—we didn't get any from him. Instead, this urbane, sophisticated man lifted our wounded spirits with words spoken quietly, almost to himself. He said, "In all my years of ministry, whenever the going gets rough because of preaching and living the gospel, I just turn my mind to my Lord. And when I think of *Him,* and all He went through—the ridicule, the misunderstanding, the betrayal, and then the cross—for *me,* for old me, I can't get too worked up about what I may be going through at the moment. I just think of my Lord—and it helps."

Our friend left town that evening and we didn't see him again, but his words stayed with us. They were like good seed in our hearts. Help had come gently, but unmistakably. Thinking of our Lord during our time of suffering made the wounds easier to bear. Looking at Him got our eyes off ourselves and gave us perspective.

We had lived through a difficult time—no, more than lived through it. We felt not only alive but strong . . . and very much at peace.

While that particular phase seemed over, and a beautiful new work of the Spirit was begun, the experience had left scars deep inside me. I wasn't aware of them until much later.

It happened on a rare quiet afternoon at our house. Everyone else was off somewhere, and I was about to splurge on an afternoon to myself. I was savoring the time to read . . . about five books I had already begun stared at me from my bed stand. I reached for the smallest one, a slim volume on praise, hoping I would have the satisfaction of finishing it. I read for most of the afternoon and I was almost at the end of the book when a feeling of excitement came over me. I was expectant, eager, as if something important was about to happen. As I read I came to a quote from 1 Thessalonians 5:16–18: "Rejoice evermore. Pray without ceasing. In every thing give thanks: for this is the will of God in Christ Jesus concerning you" (KJV).

The words seemed to speak directly to me, and in response I began thanking God for all the beautiful and happy things in my life:

For my husband. . . . What do you say when, after twenty-two years of sharing life, you feel more love than when you first began — not *less,* but *more!* And not just love, but its handmaidens: Honesty and freedom of expression . . . the things that stretch a relationship and allow the soul within to grow. I thanked my God for Lou.

For our children, each one so unique, so full of his and her own special brand of joy and potential. I almost ached with love as I thought of Dan, Tim, Andie, and Jim. . . .

For my mother's healing . . . because now this wonderful woman who had worked so hard — and alone — to raise a daughter would have a chance to enjoy her retirement years with her good husband. . . .

For Louie's parents — so incredibly active and used by God in their "retirement" ministry. . . .

For our special friends, the ones we call our "warm fuzzies," the ones with whom we share our life and ministry. . . .

For our congregation . . . if our first years among these people were hard, the recent years more than made up for them. We were among a loving, ministering core of believers, sharing their faith and trying to live the gospel we all believed in. . . .

There were so many things to thank God for . . . they kept coming to my mind, one after another. I had never known such a full heart. But when I thought I was through, the Spirit let me know that He was not through with me . . . I heard no words, but the feeling was very clear—*There is more!*

In my mind I answered, "But, Lord, I've thanked You for *everything*—for *all* the good and lovely things in my life—honestly!"

Again there was that feeling—*There is more!*

I went back to 1 Thessalonians 5:16–18—". . . In every thing give thanks: for this is the will of God in Christ Jesus concerning you." And again the words seemed to speak directly to me. They weren't telling me to thank God for all the beautiful and lovely things in my life. They said, ". . . In *every* thing give thanks. . . ." *All things.* . . . Did that mean even the hard, the painful things? Was I to thank God for the times of suffering, too? Yes—that was the "something more." The Spirit seemed to confirm it in my heart.

Now, if you were like me, you'd be thinking, "Wait a minute—that would be insincere. It doesn't make sense." To thank God for the good that comes out of suffering is realistic—but to thank Him for the suffering itself—well, I just didn't understand. Yet I knew that there were times when I had to respond to God in a simple, childlike way, or my faith wouldn't work. This was one of those times.

And so I began—thanking God for all the hard and bitter experiences of the past years. One by one, I relived them, and as I named them aloud they seemed so petty . . . the letters, the phone calls, the looks. As God brought them into my mind I was able to let go and give them to Him — with thanks. Then it was finished, and I was spent. But I felt whole. Deep inside me something tender had been touched by a gentle, loving, healing Hand. While I still didn't understand what had happened, I knew that thanking God in all things had done something for me that I wasn't able to do for myself. Yes, I felt a kind of joy. . . . I knew then that this final Beatitude was as real, as practical, as right for today as all the others.

As the burden was lifted from my heart, I felt love replacing it . . . love for those who had helped, forgiveness and love for those who had hurt . . . understanding for their motives, compassion for their prejudices. I was free . . . and the kingdom of heaven was mine.

*Happy is the woman who knows that God stands with her in times of suffering and persecution. This woman can be unjustly criticized and won't jump to her own defense . . . she can take slander without lashing back . . . she can even accept the misunderstanding of friends. She can do all these things because of Christ. When there is bitterness in the deepest parts of her heart, she asks Him to take it from her. At that moment, when she can say, "Bless them, Lord, for they know not what they do," the kingdom of heaven is hers.*

# 9

_____

You are the earth's salt. . . . You are the world's
light. . . .

Matthew 5:13, 14 PHILLIPS

Ye are the salt of the earth: but if the salt have
lost his savour, wherewith shall it be salted? it
is thenceforth good for nothing, but to be cast
out, and to be trodden under foot of men.
Ye are the light of the world. A city that is set on
an hill cannot be hid.

Matthew 5:13, 14 KJV

# The Salty Christians

I've just come in from another walk along the beach. This
time my body doesn't tingle from the chill winter wind . . .
now I'm warmed by the sun, for it is the eve of summer.

When I started out this morning I was thinking about the
words that follow the Beatitudes. . . . "You are the earth's
salt," Jesus said to His followers. And I wondered if He was
saying, "If you live these Beatitudes, then you _will_ be like
salt to the earth."

As I wondered—and walked—I found myself on a lonely
stretch of beach . . . no surfers, no sun worshipers, absolutely

117

no one but me. Suddenly I had a delicious urge . . . with the sun warm on my back I wanted to run into the sea. I wanted to let the waves wash over my tired body and clear the haze from my mind. Ordinarily my children have to pull me into the ocean unless the water is lukewarm, but today my need for refreshment was greater than my desire for creature comfort. I wasn't dressed for the occasion, but my shirt and shorts were expendable. In I went.

It was wonderful! Laughing, squealing, feeling the swells lift me and then being tumbled about by a breaking wave . . . for a few lovely minutes I was fourteen again! But the best part was coming out of the water, my clothes dripping wet, and plopping onto a warm bed of sand. Pure joy . . . one of the best feelings in the world, and today it was mine!

Lying there, I could taste the salt around my mouth. Here and there on my arms and legs were little telltale spots of white. Salt . . . salt. . . . What was Jesus telling us?

We take so many things for granted in our world that sometimes we lose sight of their real value. Surely salt is one of these. It's essential, yet very ordinary. We see it on every table, every cook uses it without even thinking about it. Still, there must be something special, something meaningful about it.

Again, it helps me to imagine myself back in the days when Jesus spoke these words. Yes, already there is more substance to *salt*—for in those days you couldn't just pick up a box of salt (iodized or plain) off your supermarket shelf. Salt came from great distances, carried on the backs of camels in long caravans along dangerous routes. Since there wasn't a lot of it, it was used carefully. It was expensive and people paid the price, because no one could do without it. Salt was essential to purify, preserve, and flavor food. There were no refrigerators in those days, no tin cans or sealed packages—in fact, there wasn't very much food. And without salt, there might be starvation.

Purity, preserving, flavor . . . perhaps these are also the qualities of a "salty" Christian. . . .

*Purity* . . . in a world that has abandoned many of its moral standards, the salty Christian will hold onto God's loving guidelines—not because he *has* to, but because he *wants* to. He knows that God's Way is the only way to a better life.

During the past few years several young people have lived in our home—sometimes for a few days or a week, and sometimes for a year . . . some for happy reasons and some for sad ones. No matter who, or why, or for how long, each one left the special gift of his or her personality in our hearts. One of them, after struggling to make sense out of the changing moral values she found in her world, came to this conclusion: "Not from a sense of 'oughtness' or 'shouldness,' but from a purely practical approach, God's ways are best." She was becoming a salty Christian. . . .

*Preserving* . . . we preserve things to keep them from rotting, from souring, from going bad. That's why Jesus wants us to be like salt rubbed into society to keep it from going bad.

How's that for a challenge! In a world like ours, where do we begin? I guess the best place is right where we are . . . in our homes, in our community. We have to begin by making contact with people. We have to get involved in the events that concern us. We can't hide in the church and mingle only with our Christian friends.

We won't always be comfortable out in the world. . . . The rubbing in of salt may rub us, and others, the wrong way. And we must be willing to be used up. . . .

Two friends of mine, both of them devoted mothers, had a close brush with the drug problem in our town. It happens to many parents, and many turn and run scared. Not these women . . . they wanted help for their own children, yes, but they also wanted it for all children. So they did something about it . . . they went to the head of the Probation Department, the head of the Welfare Department, and the Chief of Police, and with their help and support they set up a Youth Services Bureau for kids with a drug problem—or any other kind of problem. And now, thanks to these two salty Christians—and to God, to whom they give all the credit—a lot of our young people are being "preserved."

We don't have to look far to find the spots that need salt. And as we are used up, we'll be replenished . . . there is no end to the supply, for our Source is inexhaustible.

*Flavoring* . . . now, this use of salt is the easiest for me to understand. I love to cook, to spice things up, and of course I couldn't get along without salt. In fact, any complaints I get in the cooking department are usually, "Hey, Mom, a little heavy on the salt, don'cha think?" Salt brings out the flavor of food and sometimes I overdo it . . . but when I use just the right amount—ah, how it enhances the meal!

Jesus said that we Christians are to be to life what salt is to food. We are to add flavor and spice . . . to be real people, full of fun and joy.

Robert Louis Stevenson once wrote in his journal, "Went to church today, and was not greatly depressed." Ouch! Bland, flavorless people *can* be depressing, and Christians are the last people in the world who should be that way. We should be the happiest people because we worship a living Lord . . . and when the worship service is over we should carry our joy with us into our daily service out in the world.

I don't like to see blandness in the church. It makes people think that God squeezed all the fun out of the life we gave to Him. He certainly didn't . . . in fact, He introduces us to a deeper level of joy.

In our congregation we have a real swinger . . . an outgoing, warm, delightful woman named Tony. During the past year she opened up her life to Christ, and I'm happy to say that she is still a swinger . . . she just swings in a new

direction. Tony radiates so much energy and gaiety that it's
fun just to be around her. She's salty . . . in the way that every
Christian should be.

The sun's healing rays drenched me with warmth . . . its
light was so bright in my eyes that I had to roll my head from
side to side. It reminded me that Jesus also said, "You are
the world's light. . . ."

Jesus, *You* are the Light of the world . . . yet here You are,
telling us to glow. If You mean we should generate our own
light from within . . . well, I just can't do it. I don't have what
it takes. If I am to shine, I'll have to borrow light from You.
. . . My life will be Your lamp.

Somewhere I read that the houses in ancient Palestine were
very dark because they each had only one small window. A
lamp was simply a bowl filled with oil and a floating wick, and
it was kept on a lamp stand in a prominent place in the house.
Remember . . . there weren't any matches in those days and
relighting the lamp was pretty difficult, so lamps were left
burning most of the time. When people left the house they
placed an earthenware bushel measure over the lamp which
allowed it to burn safely while they were away. But when
they returned, the lamp was immediately uncovered so that
it could bring light to everyone in the family.

That's what Jesus is telling us to do . . . to keep our light
in the open where it can be seen—and where it can help
others to see. In other words, if we are going to live the
Beatitudes, we must do it openly . . . this is where privacy
ends. Our light must burn brightly in our attitude toward our
fellow human beings.

Light is a powerful force that pushes back the darkness. But
there are places where light will not go . . . it stops at a closed
door. And so must we. We can go just so far. Some people will
resist our faith . . . some will run from Jesus . . . some have

been in darkness so long they're afraid of the Light. It's right for us to push back the darkness, to bring God's light out into the world, but we have to respect the closed door. The individual will is the key to the door—and only the person whose will it is can open it . . . and when he does we can be ready to flood the area with His brightness.

Light has a nourishing quality . . . when I think of plants seeking the sun, I realize that light helps living things to grow. So it is with the light-filled Christian who shares his faith with those around him. He gives them food for the growing spirit. . . .

Today there are a lot of windows in our houses. We push a button and our homes are flooded with light . . . dimmer, brighter, whichever we choose. We have soft lights and highlights. Many things have changed, but we human beings are still the same. We still need the Light of the world. And we especially need Him in our homes.

How important it is for a mother and father to be light-filled Christians . . . to give their children an environment of warmth and nourishment where they can grow into the persons God wants them to be. How important for a husband and wife to give light to each other, for they too must continue to grow as loving human beings. Sometimes, when I'm weary from stretching, from growing, I see the light of my husband's faith and it gives me energy. Hopefully my light reaches him as well.

And there are others who need our light . . . our friends, the people we work among, our neighbors in the world. If we meet them in an attitude of love, they will grow . . . and so will we. I've seen it happen. . . .

Fred Williams is a member of our church executive staff. Thirteen years ago he came to our town after graduating from a black university in the South where he was trained as a teacher. Then he learned that teaching wasn't really what he wanted to do. He had a large family to support, so he took whatever job he could get, and he became our custodian. He was a good one — and he had other talents as well.

In the years that followed, some of our key lay people and staff realized that Fred Williams was capable of taking on executive responsibilities. So, when our business administrator died, Fred was made Building and Property Administrator. He is responsible for budget control, building use, protection, insurance, and supervision of all church property. His judgment and recommendations are highly respected by our church officers. He has also shown a remarkable ability to work with all age groups, sometimes firmly, but always with love.

Fred continues to grow . . . as an executive, as a trusted counselor, as a Christian, as a man. Recently he said, "I've never felt so full . . . not only as a Christian in my faith, but with *all* people. The trust I feel from the staff and people here — well, it's given me confidence in myself. I feel free to *be*."

Fred grew in the radiance that came through a few light-filled Christians . . . and this is what Jesus wants all of us to do, all the time. He wants us to reflect God's love until it shines throughout the world.

"Let your light shine like that in the sight of men. Let them see the good things you do and praise your Father in Heaven" (Matthew 5:16). There is no better way for us to do this than to be the lamps for His Light. And we become His lamps — fitted and ready to transmit His Light — by letting our lives be shaped by the Beatitudes. These are the attitudes that ought to be.


As I enjoyed the last few moments of sun and sand I felt rich and full and glad. God had spoken to me about my life, my goals. I want to be a loving, sensitive wife, a freeing mother,

and a caring woman in my community. But there is more—
much more to my future. I was created to do something magnificent—and so were you. We were designed before the beginning of anything—and everything—*to bring praise to our
Father in heaven.* What a great and beautiful goal!

I stood up and brushed the sand from my arms and legs.
As I walked along the beach toward home, I felt washed by
waves of hope, expectation, love, and joy. In my heart the
Spirit whispered of the goodness of life and confirmed that
the best was still ahead. For over twenty years I had walked—
sometimes stumbling—along the Way with Jesus. Yet so much
more was to come.

My tender skin told me that I had had enough of the sun
for one day. But my heart—newly tender from the touch of
the Spirit—told me that I had only just begun with the
Son of God.

*Happy is the woman who is used by the Lord to warm and en-
liven the human spirit . . . and whose life becomes her daily witness
to His immeasurable goodness.*